SPIRALGUIDE

Travel With Someone You Trust®

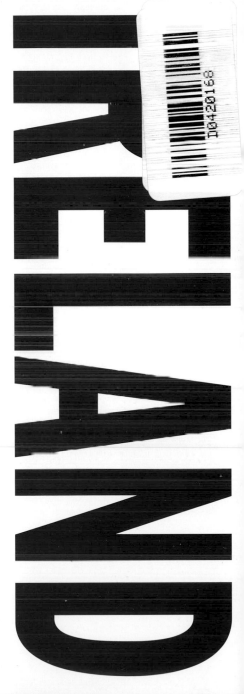

D042016B

Contents

Written by Christopher Somerville
Revised and updated by Louise McGrath

Edited, designed and produced by AA Publishing, a trading name
of AA Media Limited, whose registered office is Fanum House,
Basing View, Basingstoke, Hampshire RG21 4EA.
Registered number 06112600.

Published in the United States by AAA Publishing,
1000 AAA Drive, Heathrow, Florida 32746.
Published in the United Kingdom by AA Publishing.

ISBN: 978-1-59508-429-3

Cover design and binding style by permission of AA Publishing
Color separation by AA Digital Department
Printed and bound in China by Leo Paper Products

The Magazine

A great holiday is more than just lying on a beach or shopping till you drop – to really get the most from your trip you need to know what makes the place tick. The Magazine provides an entertaining overview to some of the social, cultural and natural elements that make up Ireland's unique character.

FAILTE IRELAND

WELCOME TO IRELAND

Over the past two decades Ireland has faced sweeping changes that have transformed its leisurely rural image into a modern European country. The old stereotypes and jokes have waned, giving Ireland the space to embrace modernity while retaining pride in its history and identity.

For generations Ireland was represented as wild, untamed and backwards, an image perpetuated by oppression and poverty. The 19th century brought emancipation for Roman Catholics in Britain, but Ireland was devastated by the Great Famine (▶ 19). As the people picked up the pieces of a ravished land, Irish nationalism bubbled under the surface and spurred the move towards self governance.

Home Rule and then independence came to the Republic of Ireland but it struggled to modernize and feed itself, while violence in Northern Ireland divided the community and isolated it from both the UK and the rest of Ireland. The country became a member of the European Union in 1973 but it took until the 1990s to see any major changes in the country. The state fuelled the pace of change by encouraging foreign investment and improving education levels. This meant that by the beginning of the 21st century, Dublin, Cork, Galway and even Belfast had been transformed from poor cities into some of the most vibrant in Europe.

Boom and Bust

What became known as the Celtic Tiger might have brought a boom in investment to the Republic of Ireland but it also included plenty of over-speculation and now the whole country is suffering the consequences. At the end of the first decade of the 21st century, difficult times have returned; recession, job losses and slumping house prices have all left their mark. The strong euro and high prices in the Republic led many people to cross the border into Northern Ireland to buy cheaper goods, particularly alcohol, though In 2010, with the euro much weaker and the sale of ultra-cheap alcohol banned in the UK, this trend started to slow.

In Northern Ireland the change was fuelled by the Good Friday Agreement as well as the UK's economic high; a larger proportion of Northern Ireland's population began to feel more prosperous, and today this means that most of the community has a stake in society and doesn't want to return to the past.

Modern Ireland

Despite the downturn, Ireland is a transformed country. Visitors have a choice of modern Irish dining and boutique hotels in the cities, or the slower pace and peat fires of rural villages. What is most apparent, though, is that Ireland has become more accessible: it's much easier to get everywhere on the network of motorways and fast roads that now connect the country from Cork and Galway to Dublin and northwards to Belfast.

Above: The state-of-the-art Victoria Square shopping centre in Belfast opened in 2008

A SPORTING NATION

If it's true that you can tell all about a country by the way it plays its sports, then Ireland is romantic, whole-hearted, crazily optimistic and remarkably successful for its size.

Watching the Best

Sports are played professionally all over Ireland, many of them attracting top-class international competitors – golf, for example, with both the Ryder Cup and Solheim Cup competitions, can boast numerous courses across the island, many in fabulous coastal locations. The Republic's soccer team has reached the finals of three world cups (1990, 1994 and 2002), while Northern Ireland's adventure in the 1958 World Cup Finals (they reached the quarter-finals) is a much-told tale. The popularity of rugby union is on the rise

> "The celebrated love affair between the Irish and their horses goes back thousands of years"

as is the quality of the game itself and the sport is sure to go from strength to strength in the coming years.

The celebrated love affair between the Irish and their horses goes back thousands of years, and Irish race meetings – especially at The Curragh in Co Kildare, one of the best-known tracks in the world – gather huge and extremely knowledgeable crowds, who bet as if stones were sovereigns.

Joining in

Professionals may catch the headlines, but games are played among friends, hard and humorously, just for the fun of it (all right, and in a spirit of healthy competition too), throughout Ireland. Beach-based sports are becoming hugely popular: kitesurfing in Cork, kiteboarding in Clare, surfing in Donegal, kitebuggying and landboarding in Derry. Country walking and hill climbing have been greatly facilitated by the development of nearly 40 waymarked ways. Fishing remains one of the great visitor attractions, too. There are also a number of country sports such as informal trotting races, and the extraordinary road bowling of south Armagh and west Cork, which involves players propelling an iron ball along a couple of miles of back country lanes in as few throws as possible – a finely developed skill.

Gaelic Games

Of the sports played in Ireland, it is the traditional Gaelic games that bind the Irish most effectively together as a nation. The two most spectacular ancient traditional sports are Gaelic football (in which players can kick and hit the ball), and hurling. To be part of a shouting, partisan crowd at a hurling match, as the players race the length of the pitch and whack the *sliotar*, or leather ball, with their club-like hurleys, is to taste true passion both on and off the field – whether you are among 80,000 at Dublin's Croke Park for the All-Ireland Final, or at a local ground way out in the sticks.

Elation after winning at The Curragh

Irish Mythology

To many, Irish mythology is a collection of tales of heroic exploits, but there are actually four distinct cycles of myths. All have had a lasting influence on Irish culture and are so ingrained in the collective psyche that they embody how the Irish see themselves.

Mythological Cycle

The Mythological Cycle, or Invasion Myths, derives from the oral tradition and ancient manuscripts. Among these is the *Lebor na hUidre* or *Book of the Dun Cow,* which includes the story of Tuan, who was reincarnated as a series of beasts and witnessed several invasions of Ireland. He recounted these stories to a Christian monk, St Finnen (Finian), who transcribed them in the 12th century.

Tuan's story recounts the arrival of the Parthalonians, Nemedians, Fir Bolgs, Tuatha Dé Dannan and the Milesians in Ireland. Each race battled with and defeated the former one, until finally the Tuatha Dé Dannan and the Milesians came to a truce. The Tuatha Dé Dannan, being a divine race, took the underworld and retreated into the passage tombs, ringforts and stone circles, eventually becoming the "fairy folk". The Milesians took the land of Ireland; many Irish families claim descent from these first Celtic settlers.

Ulster Cycle

The Ulster Cycle relies mainly on the *Táin Bó Cúailinge,* or *Cattle Raid of Cooley,* which recounts the heroic tales of Conor mac Nessa, Cuchulainn and the Red Branch Knights of Ulster, who defended Ulster against the armies of Queen Mebh of Connacht.

The seat of the High King of Ulster was at Emain Macha (Navan Fort, ➤ 165–166), near Armagh. It was named after the goddess Macha who,

The seven stone circles at Beaghmore, Cu Tyrone, were only discovered in 1945

being forced to run a race while pregnant, fell into labour and while giving birth cursed the men of Ulster: they would suffer the pains of childbirth during the time of Ulster's greatest peril.

Queen Mebh possessed the White Bull of Connacht. Hearing that the Brown Bull of Ulster was greater, she raised an army of her greatest warriors and marched on Ulster to seize the Brown Bull. Conor's elite troops belonged to a warrior band called the Craobh Rua, the Red Branch. As they mobilized to defend Ulster, they were cut down by the pangs of childbirth. Desperate and defenceless, their only hope was the semi divine warrior, Cuchulainn.

Probably the most famous of Irish mythological characters, Cuchulainn is the prominent character in *The Táin*. The son of the god Lugh and Deichtine, daughter of Conor mac Nessa, Cuchulainn was destined for fame and glory. Schooled in the art of war and possessing a magical gift of the war spasm, he was transformed into a monstrous warrior who could slay men by the dozen. His life culminated in the Cattle Raid of Cooley, where he killed Connacht's greatest champions, including his own foster brother Ferdia, who had deserted Ulster to fight for Connacht. The story of their battle is called the Combat at the Ford and stands as one of Irish mythology's greatest tales of honour, love and loyalty combined with violence, regret and bitterness.

Cuchulainn finally has to face his own fate; after many battles and after having sustained many injuries, he nears death, but he has one last lesson to teach – the ultimate display of defiance in the face of the enemy. He ties himself to a standing stone with a shield and a sword, and fights until the war goddess, the Morrigan, in the shape of a raven, lands on his shoulder and takes his soul. Unsure if Cuchulainn is dead, his enemies only approach when they see the raven drink the blood of the now-dead warrior. This image of Cuchulainn, on his feet and still defiant in death, was reproduced in art throughout the 20th century, most famously in a bronze sculpture located inside the General Post Office in Dublin (➤ 60), which commemorates the Easter Rising of 1916.

Fenian Cycle

The Fenian Cycle is drawn from a number of manuscripts and poems written from the seventh century onwards, although the stories are set in the first few centuries after Christ. The cycle revolves around an extremely elite warrior band known as the Fianna, whose principle role was to defend Ireland, led by Fionn mac Cumhaill.

Fionn's father, Cumhaill, was the head of the Clan Bascna as well as the Fianna. At the Battle of Knock, Clan Bascna was defeated by the Clan Morna, whose chief, Goll mac Morna, assumed leadership of the Fianna. Cumhaill's wife, pregnant and fearing for her life, flees into the forest, where she gives birth to a son, Fionn, who is raised in secret. There are stories of his childhood, including his attainment of the magical gift of knowledge after burning his thumb while cooking the Salmon of Knowledge for a druid. After reclaiming the leadership of the Clan Bascna, Fionn completes three tasks and is admitted to the court of the High King at Tara. There he encounters a goblin, who is terrorising Tara. He kills it with a magic spear, and for this service by Fionn to Tara, the High King, Cormac, appoints Fionn as head of the Fianna. The king demands that all the Fianna pledge allegiance to Fionn, and the first to do so is Goll mac Morna.

> "Cuchulainn finally has to face his own fate, after many battles"

The Fenian Cycle is rich with tales involving the *sidhe* (fairy folk), battles, love, treachery, glory and honour, including the birth of Fionn's son Oisín and the epic love story of Diarmuid and Grainne. The Fenian Cycle has also been used to represent Irish nationalism: the 19th century saw the emergence of the Fenian Brotherhood, an organization established to

Heroes Cuchulainn (left) and Oisin and Niamh of the Golden Hair (right)

promote and finance militant Irish nationalism; and in the 20th century, a Republic youth organization was established called Fianna na hÉireann (Warriors of Ireland).

Historical Cycle

It's hard to tell where mythology ends and history starts but what is known as the Historical Cycle comprises actual people and events. At the root of these are the High Kings of Ireland, as recorded in early Christian and medieval manuscripts, such as the *Annals of the Four Masters* and the *Annals of Ulster*.

Brian Boru is Ireland's most famous high king, perhaps because he was the first to unite all the provinces of Ireland against a common enemy, the Danes. He came from the tribe of Dál gCais (Dalcassians), based along the River Shannon in the counties of Limerick and Clare, an area still known as the Kingdom of Thomond. Brian won territory through a mixture of war and alliances, eventually becoming the High King of Ireland. He repelled the Danes at Clontarf in 1014, where he lost his life and ensured his place in Irish history. There are legends about Brian and his exploits in Ireland, including the knee harp used as a symbol of the Irish government. Known as the Tara Harp, it is kept in Trinity College, Dublin (➤ 50). Legend states it belonged to Brian Boru, but the harp dates from around 1400.

Movers and
SHAKERS

Ireland has seen her fair share of fireball personalities, from mythical heroes to real-life tyrants, political giants and singers with plenty to shout about.

St Patrick

The patron saint of Ireland was a lad of 16 when Irish pirates lifted him from his native Wales, around the time the Romans were beginning to leave Britain. After six years' enslavement as a shepherd, he escaped from Ireland, getting away to Britain on a ship loaded with a cargo of wolfhounds. Few details are known of the time Patrick spent wandering and studying in Gaul, on the Continent. He became a priest and was consecrated bishop in 432 in order to lead a mission to Ireland. Landing in County Down, he set about converting the island to Christianity. By the time he died, around 461, he had seen his message take root all across Ireland. A confrontational approach with the local chieftains and druid-priests would have achieved little except his own summary execution. But Patrick, a subtle man, preferred to work with existing sacred places and established customs, changing their focus from pagan to Christian.

Dermot MacMurrough and Strongbow

The course of Irish history was shaken forever by Dermot MacMurrough, King of Leinster, who had a year-long affair with Dervorgilla, the wife of his rival Sligo chieftain Tiernán O'Rourke of Breifne in 1152. Banished for this misconduct, MacMurrough appealed to the Norman Earl of Pembroke, Richard de Clare, aptly nicknamed Strongbow. The Normans had been waiting for an excuse to get a finger into the rich pie of Ireland, and in 1170 Strongbow came over to Ireland to help MacMurrough regain his titles, and to scoop the rewards – plenty of land, the hand of MacMurrough's daughter in marriage, and the promise of succeeding to all his father-in-law's wealth and estates. This was followed by a full-scale invasion by Norman knights, the start of centuries of Anglo-Irish friction.

Oliver Cromwell

The Lord Protector of England made it his business to come to Ireland in 1649, when it looked as if Roman Catholic rebels were getting the

upper hand over the Protestant incomers who had been granted Irish land since Tudor times. Cromwell landed In Dublin with his own dedicated army of 20,000 men and within three years of merciless campaigning the rebels had been crushed, and hundreds of thousands lay dead. The Catholic landed gentry had been forced west into the wastes of Connacht and stripped of their civil rights and property. This was a brutal slam of the door on Ireland's Catholic and Celtic heritage – but, as things turned out, not a final one.

William of Orange

Born in The Hague in 1650, William, Prince of Orange, became stadholder or sovereign of the Netherlands in 1872 after battles with Louis IV's French troops, and thereafter was seen as a champion of Protestantism. In Ireland he is most renowned for his victory at the Battle of the Boyne. This followed the Glorious Revolution in 1689, in which William deposed his uncle and father-in-law, James II, as King of England, making way for him to become William III himself. Jacobite uprisings followed, particularly In the majority Catholic Ireland where

Top: St Patrick had the satisfaction of watching Christianity flourish in Ireland
Centre: Oliver Cromwell crushed 17th-century Catholic resistance with brutal authority
Bottom: William of Orange, victor of the Battle of the Boyne

many wanted to recover lands taken from them by Cromwell. However, the Jacobite army was defeated on the banks of the River Boyne (➤ 88) on 12 July 1690 and James II went into exile for the rest of his life. William then instigated the Bill of Rights, which included a clause excluding Catholics from becoming the British monarch from thereon. The Battle of the Boyne is commemorated by the Orange Order each year, particularly in Northern Ireland.

Arthur Guinness

Ireland's international image owes much to Arthur Guinness, who in 1759 bought up little Rainsford's Brewery at St James's Gate in Dublin and started black-roasting his malt. His legacy persists in the heady malt and hop smells that waft across Dublin, and in 2.5 million white-froth moustaches gladly worn in more than 120 countries worldwide every day.

Daniel O'Connell

A 19th-century Irish political leader, Daniel O'Connell is known as The Liberator, as he fought tireless for Catholic Emancipation, the right to stand in the British parliament. He was born in Cahirciveen, County Kerry, in 1775, became a barrister, then stood and won a seat in the British parliament in a County Clare by-election. As he was Catholic, he couldn't take the seat, but he continued his battle for Catholic rights. His efforts were key in eventual Catholic Emancipation, in 1829; afterwards he fought for the repeal of the Act of Union that had merged the governments of Great Britain and Ireland in 1801, for which he was imprisoned for sedition; in the 1830s he defended a group of Catholic participants who had fought against the payment of tithes (to the Church of Ireland); and in 1841 became the first Catholic Mayor of Dublin since James II was deposed. He died in 1847 in Rome and is buried at Glasnevin Cemetery in Dublin; according to his wishes, his heart was taken back to Rome.

Michael Collins (1890–1922) and Éamon de Valera (1882–1975)

Michael Collins and Éamon de Valera, who between them oversaw the birth of an independent Ireland, were magnets for polarized opinions, icons at whose shrines bitterly divided opponents still worship. Collins led the British by the nose throughout the War of Independence, but came to see how the cause of Irish nationalism could only move forward on the back of a compromise settlement with the old enemy. The foundations for an independent Ireland were dug just as much by Collins as they were by Éamon de Valera, motivator of the hardline Irish Republican Army (IRA).

De Valera had to endure a period in the wilderness after the IRA's defeat in the Civil War (1922–23), but he came back to lead his country through its final severance with Britain.

The Two Marys

Mary Robinson's election as president of the Republic of Ireland in 1990 was a symbol of the social change that was sweeping the country. During her seven years in office she captured the high ground, going out to meet the people, saying yes to interviews, listening sympathetically to the views of northern Unionists, and throwing her weight behind Ireland's drive to modernize and develop. By the time Mary Robinson relinquished the presidency of the Republic in 1997, it had been reinvented as a dynamic focus for change. Her successor Mary McAleese, a Roman Catholic barrister born in Belfast, has proved herself to be just as effective, in a different way. 'Building bridges' has been her chosen theme, and in reaching out across the sectarian divides of her native Northern Ireland and of the wider world she has gained a very high approval rating for the way she represents their country.

Top: Arthur Guinness first sold his porter in 1778. Centre: Éamon de Valera rallied republican support at passionate public meetings. Bottom: Mary McAleese is the first woman to succeed another woman as an elected head of state.

HUNGER, HOME RULE AND HOPE

The 20th century brought Home Rule for the Republic, but in the North politicians quarrelled and sectarian paramilitaries murdered their opponents and civilians. Now, devolved government and new hope have arrived in Northern Ireland.

Famine

Hunger had always been a fact of life among Ireland's Roman Catholic poor. During the 18th century the population had quadrupled, and by the 1840s had reached 9 million – most of them living chiefly on potatoes. In 1845 the *Phytophthora infestans* fungus arrived in Ireland, and potato blight spread rapidly through the country.

At first the British government provided assistance directly, through food depots; then changed their policy, organizing relief work projects on

The Great Famine led to mass emigration from Ireland

which men, women and children laboured at often futile tasks   building unwanted roads, for example – to earn money to pay for corn meal. People died of starvation and disease: cholera, typhus, relapsing fever, infantile diarrhoea. And the potato fungus disease kept returning, in 1845, 1846, 1848 and 1849, reducing the tubers to stinking black slime.

The Great Famine of 1845–50 was an unmitigated catastrophe. Historians tell us that perhaps a million people died. Another 1.5 million emigrated to the USA, Canada and the UK, the start of a mass exodus from underfunded rural areas which continued until very recently. The famine changed the face of Ireland; the country, particularly out west, is still feeling the impact. The Great Hunger had another effect, too: it heightened anti-English sentiments in Ireland and fanned anew the flames of nationalism.

Rebellion

Through the rest of the 19th century, there were uprisings against the British: Young Ireland in 1848, the Irish Republican Brotherhood (IRB) – formed simultaneously in Dublin and New York in 1858 and also known as the Fenians – in 1865 and 1867. But it wasn't until Charles Stewart Parnell rose to prominence as a reforming Irish Member of Parliament at Westminster in the 1870s and 1880s that the Home Rule movement, which called for the establishment of an Irish Parliament in Dublin, took top place on the political agenda. The Home Rule Act was passed in 1914 and was promptly suspended for the duration of World War I.

A house ruined during the Easter Rising in Dublin in 1916

The Easter Rising

This suspension was too much for the Irish Republican Brotherhood, which initiated the Easter Rising of 1916. The rebels, numbering fewer than 2,000, took over a number of public buildings in Dublin and from the steps of the General Post Office proclaimed Ireland's independence from Britain and the birth of the Republic. Within a week the Rising had been crushed. Public opinion began to turn against the English as, one by one, 15 leaders of the rising were shot in Dublin's Kilmainham Gaol (➤ 58–59) the following month. It sowed the seed for success at the ballot box in 1918 for the republican Sinn Féin political party, whose military wing, the Irish Republican Army (IRA), began to mobilize for war with Britain.

The War of Independence

In 1919 the savage War of Independence saw the IRA pitted in guerrilla warfare against the British army. The dust settled in 1921, when a truce was followed by the signing of the Anglo-Irish Treaty, which allowed for partition of the Six Counties of Ulster from the 26 counties of the newly born Irish Free State. Radical elements in the IRA could not accept the terms of the treaty, and a bloody civil war followed. It ended in 1923 with the defeat of the IRA, after which the 26-county Republic of Ireland settled down to govern herself as a modern independent state. Meanwhile, the six counties of Northern Ireland (Down, Derry, Armagh, Antrim, Tyrone and Fermanagh) remained part of the United Kingdom.

Kerry was one of the counties that formed the partitioned state in 1921

All through the last three decades of the 20th century, the Republican paramilitaries of the Provisional IRA waged guerrilla war in Northern Ireland with Loyalist paramilitaries and the British Army. Two high-profile Northern Ireland political opponents became the very face of sectarian division and intransigence: Gerry Adams,

> "This hitherto unthinkable state of affairs has come about in the aftermath of the Good Friday Agreement"

President of the Republican political party Sinn Féin, and Ian Paisley, leader of the Democratic Unionist Party.

Nowadays Paisley's successor, Peter Robinson of the Democratic Unionist Party, heads the devolved Government of Northern Ireland as First Minister, with Martin McGuinness, Adams's second-in-command, as his Deputy. This hitherto unthinkable state of affairs has come about since the Good Friday Agreement of 1998, which officially rescinded the Republic's territorial claims on the North, proposed an elected Northern Ireland Assembly, and occasioned the release of paramilitary prisoners, the decommissioning of the Provisional IRA and Loyalist groups, and – in July 2005 – the announcement that the IRA was permanently ending its armed campaign. There have been hiccups along the way, but it looks as if Northern Ireland is in line to enjoy peace and progress.

Ian Paisley (left) and Martin McGuinness (right) at Stormont in July 2007

BEST FEST

Ireland's calendar is packed with events celebrating everything from horseracing to matchmaking, but the biggest festival of all is dedicated to the country's patron, Saint Patrick.

January

Out to Lunch Festival Belfast puts on theatre, comedy and literature events to entertain you while you enjoy a midday meal. www.cqaf.com.

February

Jameson Dublin International Film Festival Catch the best of Irish and international film screenings at various cinemas in the capital.
Tedfest Fans of the cult TV show *Father Ted* dress as priests and nuns and hop on a ferry over to Inishmore in the Aran Islands for a weekend of parties, lovely girl competitions and ecumenical matters! www.tedfest.org

March

St Patrick's Day The main celebrations take place in Dublin with the week-long St Patrick's Festival. www.saintpatricksfestival.ie

April

Irish Grand National Fairyhouse hosts races throughout the year but this attracts an international crowd. www.fairyhouseracecourse.ie

May

Northwest 200 Bikers flock to Northern Ireland for this notorious road race between Portrush, Portstewart and Coleraine. www.northwest200.org

June

Irish Derby You'll need to dress up for this annual Derby Day race at The Curragh. www.curragh.ie

July

Orangefest – 12 July Battle of the Boyne parades with flute bands and Orangemen take place throughout Northern Ireland. The biggest and best parade is Belfast city centre (avoid the Ardoyne in North Belfast, and Portadown).
Oxegen Punchestown Racecourse, County Kildare clears the way for this four-day festival of music featuring legends of rock as well as the latest sounds. www.oxegen.ie
The World Fleadh For the best in Irish and Celtic music, head for Castlebar in County Mayo, where you can catch traditional and modern variants. www.theworldfleadh.com

August

Féile An Phobail The largest community-led festival in Ireland includes a lively programme of events, from the arts to roundtable discussions in Belfast.
www.feilebelfast.com

Ould Lammas Fair This centuries-old festival sees a brisk market trade in everything from horses to dulse seaweed and yellow man sweet candy.

Rose of Tralee International Festival Entrants with Irish heritage from all over the globe flock to this County Kerry beauty pageant in the hope of winning the coveted crown.
www.roseoftralee.ie

Kilkenny Arts Festival Medieval Kilkenny offers everything from classical concerts to contemporary dance in atmospheric locations.
www.kilkennyarts.ie

September

All-Ireland Senior Football and Hurling Finals The biggest day in the GAA calendar, when the crowds at Croke Park cheer on their favourite teams.
www.gaa.ie

Galway International Oyster Festival For the ultimate taste of fresh oysters and smooth Guinness, you can't beat Galway's annual extravaganza.
www.galwayoysterfest.com

Lisdoonvarna Matchmaking Festival Singles hoping to find love head to this County Clare event and some do come home with a partner!
www.matchmakerireland.com

October

Belfast Festival at Queens This major International arts festival sees world theatre, dance, visual arts and music throughout Belfast.
www.belfastfestival.com

November

Spirit of the Voice Festival Galway City venues fill with song and the spoken word for a multicultural event that takes in everything from gospel to Gaelic culture.

December

Christmas Racing Festival Racing fans head to Leopardstown on 26 December for four days of racing.
www.leopardstown.com

Above: Fairyhouse hosts some of Ireland's most prestigious horse races

Written in the
LANDSCAPE

Most of Ireland's place names are anglicized versions of Gaelic words, though some are Viking and a few were English names from the start. The key below shows how place names are derived from Irish mythology and geography as well as the country's religious and historical roots.

There are some very common prefixes and suffixes that you'll see throughout Ireland:

Ard: lofty ground
Bally: town
Ban: fair
Beg: small
Carrick: rock
Dare/doire: oak tree
Drum: ridge
Dun: fort
Gal: foreigner/stranger
Kil: church

Knock: rock
Lis: circular earthen fort
Lough: lake
More: big
Rath: circular fort
Ros: wood in the South, peninsular in the North
Sean/shan: old
Slieve: mountain
Tully: little hill

Even from this brief list you can start to see the connection between the place name and its meaning: anything beginning with "ard" is likely to be on a small hill, while a town beginning with "kil" is likely to be developed around a church. A place with "lough" in the name will probably have a lake nearby, while near a town called "dun" there might be the remains of a fortress. Here are a few examples:

Ardpatrick: St Patrick's height
Ballynahinch: town of Hinch
Carrickfergus: Fergus's rock
Dromore: big ridge
Dundrum: fort of the ridge
Kildare: church of the oak tree

Loughbeg: little lake
Rathcormack: Cormac's fort
Roscrea: Cre's wood
Shankill: old church
Tullamore: great hill

The name **Dublin** comes from Dubh Linn, meaning black pool, referring to pool of black water that once lay beside the present Dublin Castle, around which the Vikings settled. However, the official Irish name of the capital is Baile Átha Cliath, meaning the townland of the hurdle ford.

The derivation of **Belfast** is a little more obscure: it comes from the Irish Belfeirste, meaning ford at the mouth of the River Farset (which now runs underground).

There are regional variations in spelling, and sometimes the anglicization of a name has left the root difficult to define. In the Republic of Ireland road signs are in both English and Irish, which makes things easier – and helps with pronunciation!

Road signs are often a mix of Irish and English

There are also a few names that hark back to mythological places or characters, including:

Armagh: Ard-Macha, which means Macha's height and refers to the goddess Macha (► 10–11).

Brú na Bóinne: often called Newgrange, the Irish means Palace of the Boinne, home to Aenghus Óg, the god of love (► 81–84).

Eire: the Irish name for Ireland evolved from the old Irish Ériu, Celtic goddess of the land.

Giant's Causeway: known in Irish as Clochán-na-bhFomharaigh, the stepping stones of the Fomorians (► 156).

Tara: Teamhair in Irish, which means a residence on an elevated spot, in mythology the Hill of Tara was the seat of the High Kings of Ireland or Teamhair na Rí, Hill of the Kings (► 87).

You can spend a long time exploring the many variations and derivations, but hopefully this taster is enough to arouse your curiosity and introduce you to the richness of the Irish language.

THE BARD and the HARP

LIVE
MUSIC
DAILY

Ireland is famous for the *craic*, for Guinness, for horses, for soft rain and good times...but, above all, for the astonishing genius of her sons and daughters with words and music. That such a small population can produce so many world-beaters with the pen and the harp is a marvel.

The Bard...

Even if you have never visited Ireland before, Ireland has almost certainly visited you through the written word. For such a small country, Ireland has produced an enormous number of wonderful writers, something that strikes everyone who loves a good tale or a well-turned phrase marinated in wit.

King of the walk is James Joyce (► 65), whose *Ulysses* (1922) is certainly one of the greatest novels – many say the greatest – ever written. It's huge (over 700 pages), heavy and rambling; reading it is like swimming in a salty sea of words and ideas. "The book to which we are all indebted," said T S Eliot, "and from which none of us can escape."

Poetic expressions flow through Irish writing and talk, and poets abound. Famous for polemic and satire was Jonathan Swift (1667–1745), Dean of St Patrick's Cathedral in Dublin and author of such works as *Gulliver's Travels* and *A Tale of a Tub* (► 62). W B Yeats (► 178) is still the best-known "old school" Irish poet, his work rooted in the folklore and landscape of Sligo. County Monaghan's Patrick Kavanagh is another renowned poet, with a fluid and beautiful touch. Derry-born Seamus Heaney, whose deceptively uncomplicated style has a penetrating and innovative quality, wears the crown today. And the short story – in the hands of masters such as Kerry's humorous celebrant of local heroes, the publican and author John B Keane, Cork's Frank O'Connor with his poignant fables of the War of Independence and Sean O'Faolain, or Clare's Edna O'Brien (also a celebrated novelist) – seems the ideal medium for that very Irish gift of telling a good story grippingly.

Of course the Irish have always been master storytellers. Their bards were spinning tales of the heroes Fionn mac Cumhaill and Cuchulainn, and of scheming Queen Mebh and her lust for power that led to

TWELVE GREAT IRISH READS

Last Night's Fun by Ciaran Carson
Ulysses by James Joyce
Resurrection Man by Eoin McNamee
Twenty Years A-Growing by Maurice O'Sullivan
The Country Girls, Girl with Green Eyes, Girls in their Married Bliss by Edna O'Brien
Amongst Women by John McGahern
Guests of the Nation by Frank O'Connor
The Snapper, The Van, The Commitments by Roddy Doyle

Seamus Heaney was awarded the Nobel Prize for Literature in 1995

The Irish dance spectacular *Riverdance* is popular all over the world

the epic Cattle Raid of Cooley, long before anyone in Ireland had learned to put pen to paper. Given this heritage of fireside storytelling, perhaps it's not surprising that so many great playwrights originated here: think of Oscar Wilde and Richard Sheridan, J M Synge and Sean O'Casey, George Bernard Shaw and Samuel Beckett. The Abbey Theatre founded in Dublin by Synge, Yeats and Lady Gregory is still active, and many other venues over Ireland showcase established and up-and-coming Irish playwrights.

…and the Harp

Irish traditional music is essentially music to accompany rural dancing. Jigs and reels predominate, along with the slower airs that were made to float a song on. A round goatskin drum called a *bodhrán* provides the beat and rhythm, along with guitar, bouzouki or banjo; accordion, melodeon, penny whistle and flute carry the melody, while on top skate the fiddle or uillean pipes. The Irish respect and cherish this music as vibrantly alive; but they are not afraid to experiment, even to the point of translating it altogether to jazz or rock genres, or to neo-classical arrangements for piano and orchestra. The music is tough enough to withstand these wrenchings, and versatile enough to flourish within them.

Irish traditional music has enjoyed a tremendous vogue in recent times, promulgated by stage shows such as *Riverdance*, and by the rediscovery of their traditional musical roots by rock acts such as U2 and Van Morrison, along with shock artists like The Pogues. In America the punky hardcore Dropkick Murphys pack their shows with Irish jigs and reels.

In fact this resilient music has never been away. Whatever the seesawing trends of popular music, the island's rich repertoire of traditional music has always been played with love and respect by local musicians all over Ireland.

Irish music is timeless, which is not to say it is stuck in a time warp. Turlough O'Carolan, the 18th-century blind harpist, is well respected; so are fiddler Michael Coleman and the melodeon player Joe Cooley, musicians of the early and middle 20th century who directly influenced today's generation of players. The tunes they handed down, many very old, receive new life each time they are played; each rendition is unique. And new tunes are constantly being made. As you listen – or maybe pluck up enough courage to join in – you will be launching yourself on a wonderful voyage of discovery which, if you are lucky, will go on for ever.

LIVE MUSIC

If you're in the vicinity, try these noted session pubs.

Furey's, Sligo, owned by traditional band Dervish (➤ 144).

Matt Molloy's, Westport, County Mayo, owned by Chieftains flute-player Molloy, who often plays (➤ 133).

O'Connor's, Doolin, County Clare. All the greats have played here.

O'Donoghue's, Dublin. And here too (➤ 70).

CELTIC ART
and Crafts

Ireland is renowned for its Celtic knotwork, illuminated manuscripts, contemporary design and jewellery. But there's also a wealth of other crafts from linen to lace and landscape painting, all part of Irish cultural identity.

Ancient Art in Ireland

The earliest examples of art in Ireland date are found at its most ancient building, Newgrange (➤ 81–84). The simple triple spiral found carved into its Neolithic entrance stone has been used to represent Christian trinity and the triple goddess Brigid as well as contemporary jewellery. From the Bronze Age, the spirals were developed into the interlacing patterns that we refer to as Celtic knotwork.

Christian Influence

With the arrival of Christianity in Ireland in the 6th century ad came educated monks who produced elaborate illuminated manuscripts, including the Book of Kells, now held at Trinity College, Dublin (➤ 50–53). They are the most valuable and influential artistic expression of the time, highly decorated with geometrical designs entangled with images of animals and Christian figures. The vibrant colours were sourced from roots, berries, lapis lazuli and even beetles from distant countries.

The Celtic cross also appeared in the manuscripts, with its characteristic circle around the centre of the cross. As Christianity spread, high crosses, unique to Ireland, were produced across the country. First made from wood, the later crosses were larger and carved from granite, sandstone or limestone, most with elaborate interlacing patterns: fine examples can be found at Clonmacnoise (➤ 135), as well as at Moone and Castledermot, County Kildare (➤ 87).

Left: *The Red Rose,* by Sir John Lavery (1923), in the Crawford Art Gallery, Cork
Bottom: Celtic cross, with typical knotwork design

The Irish Renaissance

In the 18th and 19th centuries new painters began to emerge, thanks to the newly formed Royal Dublin Society, Royal Irish Academy, Royal Hibernian Academy and Cork's Crawford Academy. Notable artists of the period include the portrait painter James Latham (1696–1747), landscape artist Robert Carver (1730–91), and James Brenon (1837–1907), whose paintings were reflected the hardship of many people's lives. The Irish Famine forced artists, like much of the population, to emigrate – portraitists like John Butler Yeats (1839–1922) headed for London, while landscape artists like Sir John Lavery (1856–1941) and Walter Osborne (1859–1903) went to France, drawn by the Impressionists.

Modern Irish Art

The Celtic Revival in the 19th and early 20th centuries straddled language and the arts. Influenced by Irish nationalism, Joseph Patrick Haverty (1794–864) painted works like *The Limerick Piper* while sculptor John Henry Foley (1818–74) created the statue of 'the Liberator' Daniel O'Connell in Dublin. New art institutions opened in Dublin, including the National Gallery of Ireland in 1864 and the Hugh Lane Gallery in 1908. The Hugh Lane dedicated itself to promoting Irish arts; today it is home to the reconstructed studio of renowned 20th-century Irish artist Francis Bacon (1909–92), who was influenced by Surrealist and Expressionist painters. Other notable 20th-century painters include Jack Butler Yeats (1871–1957), with his images of Irish life, Seán Keating, known for his images of the Irish War of Independence, and Dublin-born Louis Le Brocquy (1916–), whose portraits can be seen in the National Gallery.

Knots, Hearts and Crosses

Irish crafts are everywhere, although there are huge variations in quality between finely crafted and mass-produced pieces. The best examples are found in the museums, including the Tara Brooch, held at the National Museum of Ireland in Dublin (► 54). This circular, silver and gold brooch dates to around 8th century ad, and is inlaid with amber, with examples of early Celtic knotwork.

Today's knotwork adorns rings, bracelets, pendants and crosses throughout the country. Artist Jim Fitzpatrick combines mythology and Irish landscape to produce vibrant mystical works that have been reproduced as posters, cards, placemats and even jigsaws. Look also for Claddagh rings, which first emerged in Ireland in the Galway village of Claddagh and are traditionally given as a token of love (the saying goes "I give you my heart and crown it with my love"). The St Brigid's Cross, a 'lop-sided' cross with a square at the centre, has a mixed heritage that combines the pagan goddess with the Christian saint. The crosses are traditionally woven from rushes, but are now also made in wood and silver.

One of the most famous schools of lace was founded in Carrickmacross, County Monaghan, and the lace here combines muslin, netting and intricate needlework.

Above: Celtic patterns in a stained glass window in St Michan's Church, Dublin

Finding Your Feet

First Two Hours

Arriving: Republic of Ireland

Dublin, Cork and Shannon airports are the main points of entry for visitors arriving by air. Most arrivals by sea come through Dublin Port or Dun Laoghaire south of Dublin; Rosslare, County Wexford, has ferry links with the UK and France. All ports and airports have currency exchange bureaux, the major car-rental firms, and taxi ranks (fares are about five times the bus fare). Most journey times to city centres are between 15 and 60 minutes, depending on traffic.

Dublin Airport 🚇 201 D5
- To get to Dublin city centre from the airport by **car**, take M1 south.
- An **Airlink bus** leaves the airport at least every 20 minutes (moderate fare) taking passengers to the city centre via the central bus station (Busarus) and Connolly and Heuston railway stations.
- **Taxis** line up outside the Arrivals area. Fares can be expensive.

Dun Laoghaire 🚇 201 E5
- If travelling by **car** to Dublin, simply follow signs for the city centre.
- There is a frequent **Dublin Bus** service to Dublin city centre.
- **Taxi fares** range from moderate to expensive (depending on traffic).
- An inexpensive **DART** service (➤ 35) from Dun Laoghaire to Dublin runs every 30 minutes (sometimes more frequently).

Cork Airport 🚇 199 E2
- To get to Cork from the airport by **car**, take N27 east.
- **Skylink** operates two hourly routes between the airport and Cork city centre via Western Road and McCurtain Street. The cost is moderate and journeys take 10–15 minutes.
- **Taxis** are available from the rank outside the terminal building. Fares are approximately double the bus fare.

Shannon Airport 🚇 199 D4
- To get to Limerick from Shannon Airport by **car,** take N18 east.
- **Bus Éireann** runs a frequent, inexpensive airport-to-Limerick/Ennis service.
- **Taxis** from Shannon Airport to Limerick are moderate to expensive.

Arriving: Northern Ireland

Visitors arriving by air will probably fly to either Belfast International or George Best Belfast City airport. Belfast and Larne ferryports are the main points of entry for arrivals by sea. All ports and airports have currency exchange bureaux, the major car-rental firms, and taxi ranks (fares are about five times the bus fare).

Belfast International Airport 🚇 197 E4
- The journey to central Belfast takes 30 to 60 minutes, depending on traffic.
- To get to Belfast city centre from the airport by **car**, follow M2 motorway.
- **Airport Express 300 service** (moderate fare, children free) runs to Belfast city centre every 30 minutes (sometimes hourly on Sundays).
- **Taxi fares** from the airport to central Belfast tend to be expensive.

George Best Belfast City Airport and Belfast Ferryport 🚇 197 E4
- The journey to Belfast takes 10 to 15 minutes, depending on traffic.
- **Taxi fares** to Belfast city centre are moderate.

Larne Ferryport ✚ 197 E4

- The journey to central Belfast takes 30–60 minutes, depending on traffic.
- To get to Belfast city centre from the ferryport by **car**, take A8 south.
- An **Ulsterbus** service runs frequently to the city centre.
- **Taxi fares** to central Belfast tend to be expensive.
- There is a frequent **rail service** to Belfast Central railway station.

Tourist Information Offices

The central Dublin and Belfast tourist offices provide an excellent service, giving assistance with reservations and information on what's on in each city.

- **Dublin Tourism** Suffolk Street, tel: 1850 230330 or 01 605 7700 (within Ireland); 0800 039 7000 (UK); 353 66 979 2083 (from all other countries); email: information@dublintourism.ie; www.visitdublin.com.
- **Belfast Welcome Centre** 47 Donegall Place, Belfast, tel: 028 9024 6609; fax: 028 9031 2424; email: info@belfastvisitor.com; www.discovernorthernireland.com or www.gotobelfast.com.

Admission Charges

The cost of admission for museums and places of interest mentioned in the text is indicated by the following price categories.
Inexpensive under €5/£4.50   **Moderate** €5–€10/£4.50–£9
Expensive over €10/£9

Getting Around

Republic of Ireland

CIE runs bus and train services in the Republic of Ireland through its subsidiaries Irish Rail (Iarnród Éireann; www.irishrail.ie), Irish Bus (Bus Éireann; www.buseirann.ie) and Dublin Bus (Bus Átha Cliath; www.dublinbus.ie).

Dublin

LUAS, Dublin's light railway system, buzzes you round the inner city (tel: 1800 300 604; www.luas.ie). The **DART**, an efficient and moderately priced rail service, connects outer Dublin, north and south, with the city centre. **Dublin Bus** (tel: 01 873 4222) runs services in Greater Dublin, as far as the outskirts of counties Meath, Kildare and Wicklow.

Bus Services

- Tickets can be bought on the buses, but it is cheaper to buy Freedom or Rambler **multi-day tickets** from the CIE information desk in Dublin Airport, Dublin Bus (59 Upper O'Connell Street), or from one of the ticket outlets in the city.

DART (Dublin Area Rapid Transit)

- There are 30 DART stations altogether (with a western line planned); the three most central are **Connolly** (north of the river, a ten-minute walk from O'Connell Street), **Tara Street**, and **Pearse Street** (both south of the river and five minutes from Trinity College).
- **Trains** run every 5 minutes in rush hour, every 10 to 15 minutes at other times of the day.

■ **Tickets** are available singly from any DART station, but it is cheaper to buy them *en bloc* from Dublin Bus (59 Upper O'Connell Street), from some newsstands around the city or at the stations.

Taxis

■ You cannot hail or stop Dublin taxis in the street: call them by telephone (numbers in the *Golden Pages*), or find a taxi rank.
■ The main city centre **taxi ranks** are at St Stephen's Green, College Green, O'Connell Street, and Westland Row to the east of Trinity College grounds.
■ Dublin taxis are mostly metered; agree fares in advance with others.

Public Transport

All the major towns and cities in the Republic are connected by rail. Bus services run to all towns and cities, and to many rural villages. Public transport in the Republic is more efficient than folklore would have you believe. Timetables, however, particularly on the railways, become subject to creative interpretation the further from Dublin that you travel.

Railway Services

■ **Irish Rail** (tel: 01 836 6222) runs the Republic's railway services. These are efficient north and south of Dublin, but in need of investment further west.
■ The Enterprise service (**Dublin–Belfast express,** eight trains per day) takes two hours: book ahead in the high season, and for crowded last trains on Friday and Sunday evenings.

Bus Services

■ **Bus Éireann** (tel: 01 836 6111), with its distinctive red-setter logo, runs services to all towns and cities, and to many rural villages.
■ The daily **express coaches** between Dublin and Belfast are good value, and can beat the train for time if traffic conditions permit.

Tickets

■ Tickets are available from any train or bus station or online (www.buseireann.ie).
■ Under-16s and other concessionary fares can be as little as half-price of the adult fare.
■ **Irish Explorer** passes are valid on Bus Éireann Expressway and Bus Éireann city services in Cork, Limerick, Galway and Waterford, and also on Iarnrod Éireann Intercity, DART and suburban rail. They are not valid for travel on cross border services.
■ The **Irish Rover Ticket** is valid as the Irish Explorer pass and also on Ulsterbus and Northern Ireland Railways.
■ The **Open-Road Pass** is a flexible pass valid for Bus Éireann Expressway, local, city and town services.

Student Discounts

The **International Student Identity Card** gives good discounts on a number of fares including mainline rail, long-distance bus and ferry tickets – all for the price of a paperback novel. It's available from **USIT** (19–21 Aston Quay, O'Connell Bridge, Dublin 2, tel: 01 602 1906). You will need proof of your student status.

Internal Air Travel

Aer Lingus, the national airline (tel: UK 0871 718 5000; US 1-800 474 7424; Ireland 0818 365000; www.aerlingus.com), flies from Dublin to

Shannon. **Aer Arann** (tel UK: 0818 210210; Ireland 0870 767 7676; www.aerarann.ie) flies from Dublin to Donegal, Sligo, Knock, Galway, Cork and Derry, and from Cork to Belfast.

Car Ferries

Two short car ferry trips that save hours on the road are:

■ Across the Shannon (20-minute crossing, every hour every day except 25 Dec) between Killimer, County Clare, and Tarbert, County Kerry (tel: 065 905 3124; www.shannonferries.com).

■ Across Waterford Harbour (10-minute crossing, continuous operation) between Ballyhack, County Wexford, and Passage East, County Waterford (tel: 051 382480).

Driving

Driving in the Republic, generally speaking, is still a pleasure. Out of the big towns the roads are uncrowded and most drivers courteous. The further west you go, the more patience you need: roads are narrower, steeper and more twisty. Signposts take some getting used to, with distances shown in kilometres on green-and-white signs and in miles on black-and-white signs. All place names are written in Irish first, followed by the English.

Driving Essentials

■ Drive on the **left-hand side** of the road.

■ Drivers and front seat passengers must wear **seat belts**, and so must rear-seat passengers if belts are fitted.

■ The **speed limit** in the Republic is: motorway (blue) 120kph/75mph; national roads (green) 100kph/62mph – in some areas 80kph/50mph; regional and local roads (white) 80kph/50mph; urban roads 50kph/31mph.

■ The **legal alcohol limit** is 0.08 per cent (80mg) alcohol per 100ml blood.

Renting a Car

■ **Fly-drive** or **rail/sail-drive** packages offer the best deals. Book ahead, mid-July to mid-August, or you may not get a car.

■ **Prices** are half as much again during high season; they usually include third party, fire, theft and passenger indemnity insurance, as well as unlimited mileage and VAT (value added tax). You will have to pay a deposit.

■ You will need a **full valid driving licence** of your country of residence, held for two years without endorsement. The age range is generally 25–70.

Bringing Your Own Car

■ You will need a **motor registration book** (with letter of authority if car is not registered in your name), a **full driving licence** or international permit and a Green Card or **insurance certificate**, valid for the Republic of Ireland.

■ No Irish resident is allowed to drive your car, apart from garage employees.

Leaving Dublin

■ M1/N1 to Dublin Airport, Drogheda, Dundalk and Belfast

■ N2 to Ashbourne, Slane and Derry

■ N3 to Navan, Cavan and Enniskillen and Sligo

■ M4/N4 to Kinnegad (where N6 leaves for Galway), to Longford (where N5 leaves for Westport), and on to Sligo

■ N7/M7 towards Portlaoise (where N8/M8 leads to Cork) and on to Limerick.

■ N11/M11 to Bray, Wicklow, Wexford and Rosslare car ferry

Northern Ireland

Belfast
Bus Services
- **Metro** (tel: 028 9066 6630; www.translink.co.uk) operates buses within the city of Belfast.
- Buy tickets in **Europa Bus Centre** (Glengall Street) or **Laganside Bus Centre**, near Central railway station (Oxford Street) or on board buses. Multiple tickets/concessions are available.

Taxis
Find taxi firm numbers in *Yellow Pages*. Black "London" cabs with yellow identifying discs are metered; others may not be. Taxi ranks are at Yorkgate and Central railway stations, at both bus stations and at City Hall.

Public Transport
Public transport in Northern Ireland is reasonably priced and well run. For information on ticket deals and student discounts ➤ 36.

Railway Services
- **Northern Ireland Railways** (tel: 028 9066 6630; www.translink.co.uk) runs a service from Belfast to Larne (Yorkgate Station, tel: 028 9074 1700), and to Derry, Bangor and Dublin (Central Station, tel: 028 9089 9400).
- Buy **tickets** at stations. For **discounts**, contact Northern Ireland Railways, or book via the Translink website, www.translink.co.uk, which often offers discounted trips.

Bus Services
- **Ulsterbus** (tel: 028 9066 6630; www.translink.co.uk) runs services to all towns and most villages across Northern Ireland.
- Buy **tickets** at bus stations or on board buses. For cheap round-trip fares, unlimited travel tickets, bus/rail options, and concessionary fares, contact Ulsterbus.
- See the Translink website for a travel planner covering Metro, Ulsterbus and train services in Northern Ireland.

Driving
Road surfaces tend to be better than in the Republic and signpost distances are given in miles only. The same rules and laws apply as in the Republic, with the legal alcohol limit at 80mg alcohol per 100ml blood.

Renting a Car
Requirements as for the Republic (➤ 37), except that you need only have held a driving licence for one year. If you plan to drive in both the Republic and Northern Ireland, check that your insurance covers you.

Bringing Your Own Car
No documents are needed, apart from a **driving licence**, by those arriving with a car by ferry from the UK or by road from the Republic of Ireland.

Leaving Belfast
- A2 north up the coast to County Antrim and the Giant's Causeway, east through Bangor and round the Ards Peninsula
- M2/A6 to Derry
- M1 to Dungannon/A4 to Enniskillen
- M1 to Junction 7/A1 to Dundalk and Dublin

Accommodation

This guide recommends a carefully selected cross-section of places to stay, ranging from luxury hotels to farmhouses. Standards of accommodation are generally high in both the Republic and Northern Ireland and prices are similar. That said, the choice of well-run, interesting places to stay is more limited in Northern Ireland.

Guest-House and Bed-and-Breakfast Accommodation

Even inexpensive **bed-and-breakfasts** (B&Bs) usually have simple private bathroom facilities and, if you want to meet Irish people and go to the places the locals like, this can be the best option. Most (but not all) B&B and **guest-house** accommodation is in the **family home**, and hosts are usually pleased to help you plan itineraries in the locality and recommend places to go for food, shopping and entertainment.

Many **specially built guest houses**, with a standard of accommodation similar to a small hotel, have been built in the last few years. The level of comfort is high, but, as the **hosts usually live elsewhere**, visitors who had hoped to stay in a family home (and sample traditional Irish hospitality) can sometimes be disappointed. It's useful to know that **food** in smaller establishments is usually limited to **breakfast**. Many hosts take pride in providing a traditional breakfast, and the best B&B or farmhouse breakfasts can beat any hotel's. As well as the full **Irish breakfast** (bacon, egg, sausages, tomato, often black or white pudding, possibly also mushrooms, served with soda bread), many places now offer a wider choice including **fresh fruits**, **fish** and **farmhouse cheeses. Freshly baked bread** or scones (biscuits) and specialities like potato bread are often served at breakfast.

Hotels

As the best guest houses provide standards of comfort that compete with that of hotels, the cost of some hotels can seem hard to justify, until the **location**, the **facilities** and, particularly, the **service** are taken into consideration. Hotel amenities have improved dramatically and many now have excellent **leisure facilities**, often including fitness centres and golf. It's always worth asking at hotels about **special offers** or short breaks, especially off season. If the price quoted is beyond your budget, never be afraid to see if the hotelier will bargain.

Booking Accommodation

Booking ahead is always a good idea. The **cities**, especially Dublin, are busy all year round. Except for the very remote scenic holiday areas, where most (but not all) accommodation closes for the winter, the **season** starts earlier and ends later than used to be the case. Summer does attract bumper crowds to seaside resorts, especially West Cork, Kerry and Galway, so an **off-season** visit can be more enjoyable. All-year pressure on accommodation in **Dublin** has made it very **expensive** and it's hard to find bargains. One solution is to use hotels such as the **Jurys Inns** (found both in the Republic and the North), which provide comfort without service and charge a **flat rate** for a room without breakfast. Further information on accommodation is available from tourist information offices everywhere or you can refer to these sources:

■ Full listings of the Irish hotels and B&Bs available can be found and booked at the **AA's internet site** (www.theAA.com).

■ The **Irish Hotels Federation** (13 Northbrook Road, Dublin 6, tel: 01 808 4419; www.irelandhotels.com) publication *Be Our Guest* lists hotel and guest-house accommodation (including Northern Ireland).

- **Town & Country Homes Association** (Belleek Road, Ballyshannon, Co Donegal, tel: 071 982 2222; www.townandcountry.ie) produces a B&B directory (€10).
- **Tourist offices** also have a range of specialized directories for other types of places to stay, including ones that cover self-catering and farmhouse accommodation.
- The **Northern Ireland Tourist Board** (www.discovernorthernireland.com) publishes a series of free accommodation guides, including hotels and guest houses, bed-and-breakfasts, budget accommodation and self-catering.
- The **Irish Farmhouse Holiday Association** (tel: 061 309955; www.irishfarmholidays.com) provides traditional hospitality and a taste of rural life.

Accommodation Prices
Expect to pay per night for a double room

€ under €70/£60   €€ €70–€130/£60–£100   €€€ over €130/£100

Food and Drink

Eating well can be a highlight of a visit to Ireland. Good-quality local ingredients, such as Galway oysters, Dublin Bay prawns, Atlantic salmon, Connemara lamb, Tyrone cheese and organically grown vegetables and herbs have become a point of pride, and there's no shortage of talent among Irish chefs. At its best, whether it's a special meal or simple pub food, eating out in Ireland is very often a satisfying combination of genuine hospitality, high standards and value for money.

International Cooking
International cooking styles tend to predominate over local tradition in a way that many visitors can find disappointing, and you are far more likely to find various world cuisines than traditional Irish food. When well produced this cosmopolitan food is fun, vibrant and tasty, but often it's just a muddle.
- **Hotel dining-rooms** are emerging as serious contenders in the restaurant stakes as many have taken on top-class chefs. The accommodation recommendations reflect this, including the Clarence and Merrion hotels in Dublin (► 68–69), and many examples around the country.
- There is a shift towards buzzy, informal **cafés and bars** serving colourful, cosmopolitan fare. Lively, efficiently run bistros and brasseries such as Zaks in Cork (► 113) and Apartment in Belfast (► 167) provide value for money, as do cafés like Dublin's stylish Bewley's Oriental Café, where drink (often coffee rather than alcohol) is the main attraction and cakes and light meals are a tempting optional extra.

Irish Cooking
Until the 1990s Irish dishes such as *colcannon* (mashed potatoes and green cabbage, seasoned with chives), *boxty* (filled potato pancakes), Dublin coddle (a stew made with sausages, bacon, onions and potato), Irish stew and corned beef with dumplings and cabbage were most likely to be found only in pubs. With a few notable exceptions, restaurant chefs felt that traditional Irish dishes were too plain, but this is changing. With the active

support of the **Restaurant Association of Ireland** (11 Bridge Court, City Gate, St Augustine Street, Dublin 8, tel: 01 677 9901; www.rai.ie) and **Bord Bia** (the Irish Food Board), many of Ireland's top chefs are now working on the concept of a **New Irish Cuisine**. Though light and modern, it is based on traditional ingredients, including many **artisan Irish food products**, such as farmhouse cheeses and smoked Atlantic salmon.

■ **Bord Bia** has produced a New Irish Cuisine **recipe booklet** (tel: 01 668 5155 for details).

■ Much of the country's best food is produced by owner-chefs in **family-run restaurants** and country houses.

■ **Kinsale** in County Cork started the first Good Food Circle in the early 1970s and, since then, many others have flourished. There is also an annual themed Kinsale Gourmet Festival.

■ **Kenmare** (County Kerry) has two of the country's finest hotels – Sheen Falls Lodge (tel: 064 664 1600; www.sheenfallslodge.ie) and Park Hotel Kenmare (tel: 064 664 1200; www.parkkenmare.com) – and the most concentrated collection of fine restaurants, quality accommodation and good pubs.

■ Other culinary hotspots around the country include **Dingle/An Daingean** (County Kerry), **Clifden** (on the Connemara coast), **Carlingford** (at the foot of the Mountains of Mourne), **Athlone** (right in the centre of the Republic) and **Moycullen** (just outside Galway), all of which have something exciting to offer.

A Practical Guide to Eating Out

The following tips give practical information to make eating out in Ireland an enjoyable and carefree experience.

■ **Eating hours** are: breakfast from about 7:30 or 8 to 10 or 10:30; lunch from noon or 12:30 to 2:15 or 2:30; early dinner (often especially good value) from 5:30 or 6 and main dinner from about 7:30 to 9:30 or 10:30.

■ There is no specific **service charge** – it can be anything from 10 to 15 per cent, or discretionary.

■ Many restaurants offer **early evening menus** (usually up to 7pm), which are very good value. Where lunch is available at leading restaurants, it's usually a bargain.

■ **Dress codes** are increasingly relaxed and very few restaurants will insist on male diners wearing a jacket and tie, although many people like to create a sense of occasion when dining out and feel more comfortable with a little formality.

■ The key **language** on menus throughout the country is English, although some will include an Irish version. A few enterprising restaurants (especially near the Shannon, which attracts holidaymakers and fisherfolk from Europe) offer menus in several European languages.

■ For further reference, Tourism Ireland produces a **restaurant directory**, *A Flavour of Ireland.* For Northern Ireland you can access the *Taste of Ulster* guide (www.tasteofulster.org).

Restaurant Prices
Expect to pay per person for a meal, excluding drinks and service

€ under €15/£12   €€ €15–€30/£12–£24   €€€ over €30/£24

Shopping

It would be hard to imagine a visit to Ireland that didn't include at least a little light shopping. The traditional goods for which the country is famous are in the main high-quality classics that will give years of pleasure. Much to the surprise of those who have been making and selling them for generations, many have recently become fashionable too.

Irish Classics

As natural fabrics and country looks become more desirable, Irish **tweeds**, **linen** and **hand-knitted sweaters** are suddenly "must-haves" for discerning shoppers from all over the world. This turn of events has resulted in a new generation of all kinds of goods with verve and style: for example, Irish **crystal** manufacturers have commissioned designers such as John Rocha to create high-fashion contemporary designs that appeal to a younger, more design-conscious shopper. The same applies in other areas: Louise Kennedy, for example, designs **clothes** for the international market but the roots of her inspiration are firmly Irish.

Where to Buy Irish Classics

Dublin has the biggest selection of shopping options anywhere in the country; notably, Irish fashions, antiques, books, handicrafts, food and drink. **Cork** is smaller and more selective, but is particularly enjoyable for shopping and has a number of outlets selling outstanding food. **Galway** has a good range of small galleries, boutiques and specialist shops, and is renowned for books.

■ **Crafts** of internationally high standard are widely available across the country and you can often find something special at one of the many craft workshops.

■ **Antiques** can still be a good buy in Ireland, although the days of easy-to-find bargains have gone. Belfast, Dublin, Cork, Galway and Limerick are all good browsing grounds, and it's worth checking the newspapers for auctions, which are often held outside the cities.

■ **Jewellery** is worth considering. Check out the antiques shops, but also look at modern designer jewellery (see Kilkenny ➤ 92 and Belfast ➤ 170) and the traditional Irish wedding rings called Claddagh rings (see Galway ➤ 143).

■ Irish cut **lead crystal** has been produced since the 18th century and is world famous. For generations the best-known manufacturer was Waterford Crystal but their glass is not currently made in Ireland. You can still buy their produce in deptartment stores and gift shops all over the country as well as the visitor centre in Waterford (➤ 85). Other hand-cut crystals, from Dublin, Cork, Kinsale, Tipperary, Galway and Tyrone, are less expensive, and there is also interesting contemporary uncut crystal, such as Jerpoint (➤ 92).

■ **Traditional Irish foods** are much sought after. Foods that travel well include smoked salmon; make sure it's wild **Atlantic salmon**, not farmed, and buy it vacuum packed. The firmer, milder, whole handmade **farmhouse cheeses** such as Gubbeen, Durrus and Cashel Blue are also a good buy; they are widely available in delicatessens, specialist cheese shops and supermarkets, and at airports (where you pay much more).

■ **Irish whiskey** has great cachet. A tour of one of the distilleries – Old Jameson Distillery, Dublin; Old Midleton Distillery, County Cork (➤ 108); and Old Bushmills Distillery, County Antrim (➤ 163) – will include a whiskey tasting, and you can buy some unusual blends on site. The well-known brands, like Jameson, Paddy, Powers and Bushmills, are widely available. **Baileys,** now one of the world's top-selling drinks, was created to make the best possible use of ingredients plentiful in Ireland – cream and whiskey. Along with **Irish Mist,** a sweetish liqueur made from whiskey and honey, it is widely available.

■ **Knitwear** is highly popular and everything from chunky Aran sweaters to sophisticated fashion knits are on offer. Every craft shop in the country has something of interest.

■ **Linen** is a great luxury, but well worth the price, being wonderfully hardwearing. Most linen is made in Northern Ireland (➤ 170). As well as the classic table- and bed-linen, linen can also be used in high fashion, as seen in designer clothes shops such as Kilkenny in Dublin (➤ 69).

■ **Tweeds,** too, never date. The best buys are classics such as men's jackets, although more contemporary-styled clothing is becoming increasingly popular. Many craft shops stock tweeds, and there are specialist shops around the country (see Magee's ➤ 144), as well as in the major cities.

Opening Times
Opening hours are usually 9 or 10 until 5 or 6:30 Monday to Saturday for mainstream shopping, with limited Sunday hours and, in cities, late-night shopping until 8pm on Thursday. In country areas, some shops still close for a half day (Wednesday and Saturday are most likely), and craft shops in holiday areas have variable hours. Browsing is quite acceptable: although assistance will usually be offered, pressure to buy is the exception.

Payment
Credit cards are widely accepted, except in small craft shops.

Entertainment

Irish entertainment most often takes the form of festivals (devoted to just about everything, ➤ 22–23), sporting events and music. Bord Fáilte (the Irish Tourist Board) and the Northern Ireland Tourist Board jointly produce a calendar of events, which is worth having if you're spending some time in Ireland. Bord Fáilte also produces booklets on golf, cycling, hiking, fishing, sailing, tracing your ancestors, literary Ireland, wildlife and many more. These are available from larger tourist offices. There are similar publications relating to Northern Ireland. Detailed information on sport and entertainment is available daily in the local press and, for advance information, the internet is a useful tool.

Spectator Sports
■ **Horse racing** is central to Irish sporting life. There are 27 racecourses and races are held most days. Major events are well publicized; for information contact **Horse Racing Ireland** (tel: 045 455455; www.goracing.ie).

■ **Greyhound racing,** held at night, is enjoying a revival, and Irish dogs are highly regarded internationally; ask locally about events.

■ Ask about local venues for **Gaelic football** and **hurling,** both fast and exciting games.

Outdoor Activities
■ **Golf** brings many visitors to Ireland. There are over 400 golf courses in the country, including many world-class championship courses. The Republic of Ireland's golfing association, the **Golfing Union of Ireland** (Unit 8, block G, Maynooth Business Campus, Maynooth, County Kildare; tel: 01 505 4000; www.gui.ie) can supply information.

■ **Hiking** is increasingly popular; long-distance paths are indicated by trail markers and signposts. The longest in the south is the Kerry Way (214km/133 miles); Northern Ireland's 800km (496-mile) Ulster Way, a circuit round Northern Ireland and County Donegal, is an even greater challenge, but splits into a number of shorter Waymarked Ways, ranging from 32km (20 miles) to 52km (32 miles).

Pubs and Clubs

■ Increasingly strict drink-driving laws have forced pubs to diversify, and many now serve **food**, at least at lunch-time. A no-smoking policy has been introduced in all enclosed places, including pubs and clubs.
■ **Music in pubs** is usually free if it's in the main bar, but amplified music and/or dancing in a separate room usually has an entrance fee. Impromptu sessions are still widespread, but music is increasingly organized and, to the chagrin of many people, even small pubs are introducing amplification.

Festivals

Consult newspapers and check your hotel room and the Tourist Information Offices for local guides to what's on (▶ 22–23). During National Heritage Week (the last full week of August) there are special events at locations across the country (www.heritageweek.ie).

Dublin

■ Dublin's festival season begins with the **Jameson Dublin International Film Festival** (mid-February) and the **St Patrick's Day Festival and Parade** (around 17 March), followed by **Bloomsday** (16 June), **Kerrygold Dublin Horse Show** (early August), **Dublin Theatre Festival** (early October) and **Dublin City Marathon** (late October).
■ The **All-Ireland Finals of Hurling and Gaelic Football** are held at Croke Park in September.

Galway

■ Kinvarra holds a traditional boat gathering, **Cruinniu na mBad** (Galway Tourist Office tel: 091 537 700), in early August, and also in Kinvarra you can attend **literary banquets** themed on local writers, including W B Yeats and Sean O'Casey, in the medieval Dunguaire Castle (tel: 061 360788; www.shannonheritage.com).
■ Galway's festivals include **Galway Arts Festival** (tel: 091 509700) in mid- to late July, followed by **Galway Races** (Ballybrit, tel: 091 753870), then the September **oyster festivals**. Clifden's **Connemara Pony Show** is in August.

Belfast

■ Belfast is really buzzing all the time these days, with events at the Waterfront Hall, the Grand Opera House, King's Hall, Ulster Hall and numerous theatres, as well as the Odyssey science centre and entertainment complex.
■ Northern Ireland's cultural highlight is the **Belfast Festival** at Queen's University, a mixture of film, theatre, music and dance in late October to early November.

Gay and Lesbian Nightlife

■ **Dublin's** best bets for LGBT drinks, DJs, concerts and drag acts include Pantibar on Capel Street, The George and The Dragon, both on South Great George Street, and Q+A at Andrews Lane Theatre.
■ In **Belfast**, try Kremlin on Donegall Street, the Union Street Bar, Mynt in Dunbar Street, Slide on Ann's Street or Dubarrys on Gresham Street.

Dublin

Getting Your Bearings

"In Dublin's fair city, where the girls are so pretty..."
Is it that snatch of an old romantic song that attracts so many
people to Dublin? Or is it Dublin's reputation as one of the
most vibrant and fun capital cities in Europe where people
still have time for the stranger? Whatever the cause, the effect
has been spectacular. During the last couple of decades of
the 20th century, Dublin broke free of a clinging image of
shabbiness and quaintness, of being far behind the times, and
emerged as a go-ahead city – loud, joyful, affluent, with
a brashness that attracted more than it repelled.

Dublin lies low and beautiful. There are few high-rise blocks
to overshadow the historic buildings – Trinity College, the
Custom House, St Patrick's Cathedral and Christ Church
Cathedral. This compact city is easy to walk around in
a day, with the Dublin Area Rapid Transit railway
(DART) to get you out along the shores of
Dublin Bay, and the Luas light rail
system to transport you out to
the suburbs.

South of the river you'll
find the pavement cafés
and fashionable watering
holes of Temple Bar, once
a run-down area but
now Dublin's snappiest
spot that continues to
grow around Cow's Lane.
Only a stone's throw
away is Ireland's best
Georgian architecture in
the streets and squares
around chic St Stephen's
Green. North of the Liffey,
wide O'Connell Street and
the area behind it in Henry

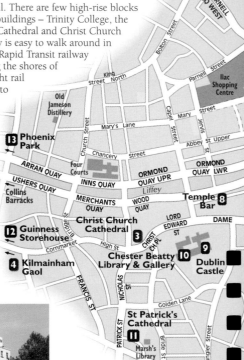

Page 45:
Looking across
Dublin's skyline
Left: The Ha'penny
Bridge

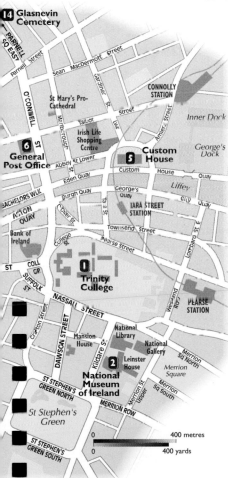

Street has had a major facelift, and Smithfield Village is taking shape as a cultural area. To the west there are street-market quarters and hidden pubs to discover. The further north and east you go, the greener, quieter and more respectable grow the neighbourhoods.

Dublin has so much going for it. There are literary connections in abundance – from old masters James Joyce and Sean O'Casey to young lions such as Emma Donoghue. Music flows through the heart of the city, from the stadium rock of U2 to the cheery good-time pub folk of bands such as The Dubliners and the energetic, sunny sound of youngsters The Delorentos.

This is a friendly city. And the friendliness is genuine, not part of some PR campaign. Enjoy it to the hilt, and then some...

In a Day

If you're not quite sure where to begin your travels, this itinerary recommends a practical and enjoyable day out in Dublin, taking in some of the best places to see using the Getting Your Bearings map on the previous page. For more information see the main entries.

9:30am

Be at **1** Trinity College (right, ➤ 50–53) bright and early, to avoid the crush in the "Turning Darkness into Light" exhibition and so get an uncluttered look at the glorious Book of Kells. Leave Trinity by the Nassau Street exit, and make your way down Kildare Street.

10:30am

Pop into the **2** National Museum of Ireland (➤ 54–56) to view the dazzling gold and jewels of ancient Ireland. Turn down Molesworth Street and cut through to reach Grafton Street, Dublin's shop-till-you-drop thoroughfare. Relax with a coffee and a sticky bun in Bewley's Café, and watch the buyers go by.

12:00noon

Stroll down the west side of St Stephen's Green and take a look at Harcourt Street's superb Georgian houses with their characteristic doorways. Then follow Cuffe Street and Kevin Street to 🔟 St Patrick's Cathedral (below opposite and left, ➤ 62–63), and stop to visit the grave of Jonathan Swift before heading northwards along Patrick Street and Nicholas Street to the older 🔟 Christ Church Cathedral and the supposed grave of Strongbow. From here it's just a 10-minute walk via Dame Street to 🔟 Temple Bar.

1:30pm

Stop for a bite to eat at **The Mermaid Cafe** on Dame Street and continue on through Temple Bar on the north side of the street until you meet the River Liffey and turn right for Aston Quay.

3:00pm

Hop on a 79 bus at Aston Quay for the 10- to 15-minute ride out to 🔟 Kilmainham Gaol (➤ 58–59), an icon of Irish history. After the tour of the gaol, make your way up the South Circular Road to the Islandbridge Gate into 🔟 Phoenix Park (➤ 64).

5:00pm

Blow away the cobwebs with an hour's saunter through the wide open spaces of Phoenix Park. You might see anything from a herd of deer to a fast-paced hurling match. Then catch the 10 bus (from NCR Gate) back to the city centre.

6:30pm

The night is yours! Start in Temple Bar, maybe, with a drink in the St John Gogarty, followed by dinner at the lively Market Bar and Tapas, perhaps, or **The Mermaid Café** in Dame Street (➤ 67). Then on to the Brazen Head or the Long Hall or Doheny & Nesbitt's or...

❶ Trinity College and the Book of Kells

Renowned as the most beautiful book in the world, the glorious and priceless Book of Kells is the unchallenged star of the show at Trinity College. These 680 pages of illuminated Latin script and painting present a virtuoso display of richness of imagination, breadth of humour and wit, and faithful observation of the world of nature, all executed with a breathtaking delicacy of touch. The monks who copied out and illustrated the four Gospels at the Monastery of Kells in County Meath around the year 800 may have learned their skill in St Columba's celebrated monastery on the Scottish island of Iona; they were certainly among the best illuminators at work in that area.

Trinity College

The Book of Kells is on display at Trinity College, an iconic Irish institution in itself. As you turn off College Street and pass through the low, unobtrusive doorway under the blue clock face, the roar of traffic fades and is overlain by the chatter of young voices and the clop and scuffle of shoes on the cobbled courtyards of Trinity College. In these peaceful quadrangles, surrounded by the mellow architecture of four centuries, you catch a sense of how Dublin must have been in a quieter age.

Not that Trinity, Ireland's premier university, is a stuffy or hidebound place these days. The college was founded in 1592 by Queen Elizabeth I "to civilise Ireland with both learning and the Protestant religion…for the reformation of the barbarism of this rude people." Up until 1966 Catholics were admitted only under special dispensation; today Trinity is completely mixed by both religion and sex (women were admitted to degrees as long ago as 1903).

The magnificently illustrated Greek letters Chi-Rho, formed from the first two letters of the Greek word for Christ, beginning a verse in Matthew's Gospel. The microscopic detail is characteristic of the Book of Kells

Emerging from the tunnel-like entrance into the cobbled enclosure of Parliament Square, you will find to your left the **university chapel**, built in 1798 to an elegant oval design. Inside, its walls are lined with rich dark wood, its ceiling stuccoed green, grey and peach. Ahead stands a tall Victorian **campanile**. If you bear right in front of it around the end of the **Old Library** (1733) you will reach its entrance. Inside, the excellent **"Turning Darkness into Light" exhibition** places the ninth-century manuscript in its historical perspective and helpfully prepares you for your encounter with the Book of Kells.

Georgian grandeur in the peaceful heart of Trinity College

The Book of Kells

The book lies under glass and the pages on show are changed every three to four months. The monks used chalk for white colour, lead for red, lapis lazuli for blue. A different shade of blue also came from woad, black from carbon and green from copper verdigris. Over the centuries, the colours on the much-admired principal pictorial pages have faded; the pages of less highly decorated script are remarkably white and well preserved. The more you look, the more you can see: sinners misbehaving, angels, ravening beasts and demons, floral tendrils, scenes wildly fantastic and touchingly domestic, conundrums of geometry that eventually resolve, as you stare at them, into initial letters.

Oscar Wilde was an alumnus of Trinity College

Other precious manuscript gospels are displayed in rotation alongside the Book of Kells: the eighth-century **Book of Mulling** and **Book of Dimma**, the **Book of Armagh** from about 807, and the **Book of Durrow**, which probably dates back to around 675 and is the oldest surviving decorated gospel book.

SIGNIFICANT STUDENTS

Illustrious Trinity alumni include: Jonathan Swift, author of *Gulliver's Travels*; playwrights Oliver Goldsmith, Oscar Wilde and Samuel Beckett; patriots and politicians Robert Emmet, Edward Carson and Henry Grattan.

High book stacks and a vaulted roof give a tunnel effect to the Long Room

The Long Room

From the Book of Kells display room, climb the stairs to reach the cathedral-like Long Room. Well over 60m (200 feet) long, this superb old library room contains nearly a quarter of a million vintage books under its wooden barrel-vaulted roof. On display here is one of the precious dozen surviving copies of the original **Proclamation of the Republic of Ireland**, whose rolling phrases were read out by Pádraic Pearse from the steps of the General Post Office on Easter Monday 1916: "…we hereby proclaim the Irish Republic as a Sovereign Independent State, and we pledge our lives and the lives of our comrades-in-arms to the cause of its freedom, of its welfare, and of its exaltation among the nations."

Nearby, on the right as you walk through the Long Room, stands a **harp** gnarled and shiny with age, beautifully carved out of dark willow wood. It can be hard to spot, its ancient brown wood camouflaged against the brown hues of the surrounding books. Unromantic carbon dating says the harp was made around 1400. But legend tells a better tale, insisting that it was once owned by Brian Boru, mightiest of the High Kings of Ireland, who fell on Good Friday 1014 at the very moment of victory over the Danes at the Battle of Clontarf.

ALERT ATTENDANTS
Make time to chat to the attendants posted around the "Turning Darkness into Light" exhibition. Not only are they friendly, they are also knowledgeable, and will point out and explain tiny details tucked away in the intricate illustrations.

TAKING A BREAK
Meander from Trinity College into Temple Bar, a district packed with lively cafés and bars. The exuberant café-restaurant **Kilkenny** is a good choice for a light lunch.

🏛 202 C3 ✉ College Street, Dublin 2 ☎ Book of Kells 01 896 2320; Library 01 896 1661; www.bookofkells.ie 🕐 Old Library and Book of Kells Exhibition: May–Sep Mon–Sat 9:30–5. Sun 9:30–4:30; Oct–Apr Mon–Sat 9.30–5, Sun 12–4:30; closed 10 days over Christmas and New Year 🚌 All cross-city buses 💷 Moderate

THE BOOK OF KELLS: INSIDE INFO

Top tip On a summer holiday weekend it can get very crowded around the case containing the Book of Kells, and you may end up with a frustratingly brief glimpse before being ushered onwards. If possible, visit on an out-of-season weekday, when you will have time to let your eyes adjust and there will be plenty of space to stand and stare.

❷ National Museum of Ireland

The National Museum of Ireland encompasses four museums, three in Dublin and one in County Mayo (▶ 133), but for many visitors the name is synonymous with the central Dublin branch, which houses the main historical collections in two separate buildings. Most visited is the Archaeology building, with its superb collection of ancient gold items, richly ornamented early Christian crosses and cups, and Viking bows.

Most of this treasure – much of it dug up by chance from peat bog or potato field – is displayed in the **Treasury** in the museum's Great Hall. There is far too much fine artistry here to take in during one visit, but try at least to see the highlights – the Ardagh Chalice, the Cross of Cong and the "Ireland's Gold" exhibits.

Gold, Silver and Precious Stones

The **Ardagh Chalice**, a heavily decorated two-handled eighth-century silver cup, was discovered by a labourer named Quinn while digging up potatoes he had planted in the ring fort of Reerasta, near Ardagh in County Limerick. Quinn, unaware of its true value, was delighted to sell his treasure trove – the chalice, some brooches, a cup and other items – for a few pounds to a local doctor. The **Cross of Cong** is a processional cross made in 1123 for Turlough O'Conor,

King of Connacht, with decorative animal heads, beaded gold wire and inlaid enamel. The magnificent eighth-century **Tara Brooch**, gleaming with amber and coloured glass and covered in intricate interlacing patterns, is the finest piece of Irish jewellery in existence, and certainly the most copied by modern jewellers.

The **Broighter Hoard**, unearthed in County Derry in the 1890s, is the Treasury's biggest collection of gold objects.

The eighth-century Tara Brooch has provided inspiration for countless pieces of Irish jewellery

Victorian ironwork frames the roof of the National Museum of Ireland

Made in the first century BC of sheet gold beaten to paper thinness, it includes a wonderful miniature boat, elaborate collars, and a string of hollow gold balls forming a necklace. Remarkable, too, are the shrines made of worked metal and wood to hold sacred objects. Among them is the 12th-century shrine of **St Patrick's Bell**, complete with the big, iron bell itself, which is early fifth century and contemporary with the saint. Legend has it that St Patrick's Bell was used to good effect when its owner climbed the holy mountain of Croagh Patrick. Attacked by a black cloud of demons, St Patrick hurled his bell at them, and they promptly disappeared.

Historical Artefacts

Other major attractions are the enormous **Lurgan log boat**, made around 2400BC, which is long enough to transport the population of an entire village if necessary; the **Viking Gallery** with its swords, pins, brooches and splendid 10th-century yew longbow; and the three galleries of the **Medieval Ireland** exhibit, documenting rural life, the nobility and religious practice from 1150 to 1550.

TAKING A BREAK

Hang out with the fashionable crowd at nearby **Café en Seine**, a great place for coffee and a bite to eat. Alternatively,

stop for a relaxed cup of coffee amid the art nouveau surroundings at a Dublin favourite, **Bewley's Oriental Café** (78 Grafton Street) and watch the shoppers as they pass by on the busy street outside.

The crafts-manship of the eighth-century Ardagh Chalice makes it one of Ireland's finest pieces of silverware

National Museum of Ireland – Archaeology
✚ 202 C2 ✉ Kildare Street, Dublin 2 ☎ 01 677 7444; www.museum.ie ⏰ Tue–Sat 10–5, Sun 2–5 🚌 7, 7A, 10, 11, 13; 172 Museum Link 🚆 Pearse Station (DART) or St Stephen's Green (Luas) 💷 Free

National Museum of Ireland – Decorative Arts & History
✚ 202, off A3 ✉ Benburb Street, Dublin 7 ☎ 01 677 7444; www.museum. ie ⏰ Tue–Sat 10–5, Sun 2–5 🚌 25, 25A, 66, 67, 90, 172; Museum Link 🚆 Heuston Station (main line); Museum (Luas) 💷 Free

---

NATIONAL MUSEUM OF IRELAND: INSIDE INFO

Top tip If you have time, make the 2km (1-mile) trip from the city centre to Collins Barracks, a handsome 18th-century building that was once used as a barracks but now houses the **Museum of Decorative Arts and History**. The collection details Ireland's social history with exhibits ranging from domestic furnishings to relics of Ireland's political martyrs, as well as paintings and sculpture.

Hidden gem Tucked away in the National Museum of Ireland is a collection of **sheela-na-gigs**, stone carvings of women uninhibitedly displaying their charms. To inspect them, you have to apply in advance to the curator.

One to miss You could afford to miss the **Egyptian exhibition** on the National Museum's upper floor; there is plenty in the Irish exhibits to keep you fascinated for hours on end.

③ Christ Church Cathedral

For a thousand years, people have come to worship at Christ Church Cathedral. First built in wood in the 11th century by Viking king Sigutryggr Silkenbeard, a hundred years later a stone replacement was ordered by the Norman Earl Strongbow, whose tomb lies alongside the pews.

It is not certain whether Strongbow is actually inside the tomb, as this is a copy – the original was crushed when the roof collapsed in the 16th century. However, beneath the alterations and renovations, most extensively in the 19th century, the Norman cathedral remains, and it is the oldest stone building in Dublin. Look out for the early 13th-century medieval stone carvings in the north transept, which depict gothic heads and musicians.

Christ Church cathedral is the seat of the Church of Ireland

Strongbow named two chapels, to Saint Edmund and Laud; in the latter you can see the reliquary heart of Archbishop Saint Laurence O'Toole, who was co-builder of the cathedral. Also note The Quire, where the archbishop's seat and organ are located, and the musician's corner, which pays homage to the 500-year-old Cathedral Choir.

Down in the crypt you can see various carved medieval stones, various gold crucifixes and religious artefacts, as well as a curious encased rat and cat, which were mummified in the organ pipes.

TAKING A BREAK

The Mermaid Cafe is on Dame Street, a 10- to 15-minute walk away, and is a great place for a light lunch or Sunday brunch.

🚻 202 A3 ✉ Christchurch Place, Dublin 8 ☎ 01 677 8099; www.cccdub.ie 🕐 Jun to mid-Jul Mon–Tue, Fri 9:45–6:15, Wed–Thu, Sat 9:45–4:15, Sun 12:30–2:30, 4:30–6:15; mid-Jul to Aug Mon–Fri 9:45–6:15, Sat 9:45–4:15, Sun 12:30–2:30, 4:30–6:15; Sep–May Mon–Sat 9:45–4:15, Sun 12:30–2:30 🚌 50 (Eden Quay), 78A (Aston Quay) 🚆 Tara Street (DART) ♿ Moderate

❹ Kilmainham Gaol

The grim but atmospheric prison of Kilmainham is a national monument that holds within its walls the key to much of Ireland's turbulent history. Here Home Rule rebels – including Wolfe Tone's United Irishmen of 1798, "Young Irelanders" of 50 years later, Fenians, and leaders of the Easter Rising – suffered imprisonment, punishment and death.

Model Prison
Kilmainham's entrance sets the tone, a thick door with a spyhatch in a massive stonework frame. Visits are by **guided tour** only and begin in the museum, introducing you to bygone Dublin and the slum conditions that bred the debt and petty crime for which most prisoners were incarcerated here. As the guide will tell you as you are taken into the great four-storey hall with its multiple floors of tiny, cold, stone cells, Kilmainham Gaol was considered a model prison when it opened in 1796. Dark corridors lead to granite stairs worn hollow by the tread of feet. Debtors, murderers, sheep stealers, rapists, prostitutes, all ended up here. Famine victims, too – during the 1840s and 1850s the gaol became overcrowded with people who had committed petty crimes simply in order to qualify for the thin but regularly served prison gruel.

Famous Inmates
You'll be shown the cells that held Pádraic Pearse, Thomas Clarke, Joseph Plunkett, James Connolly and the other leaders of the 1916 Easter Rising (➤ 20); the chapel where Plunkett and his fiancée, Grace Gifford, were married; and the high-walled yard where the leaders were shot for treason. The last prisoner to be released before Kilmainham closed in 1924 was the Republican leader Éamon de Valera (➤ 16) – later to become both head of government and president of Ireland.

The landings and cells in the gaol's grim interior

Whatever your views, you can't fail to be moved by the stories you'll hear, or by the atmosphere in this cold, echoing, haunted place. It's essential viewing for any visitor who wants to understand Ireland's recent history.

🚻 202, off A3 ✉ Inchicore Road, Dublin 8 ☎ 01 453 5984; www.heritageireland.ie 🕐 Apr–Sep daily 9:30–6; Oct–Mar Mon–Sat 9:30–5:30 (last admission 4), Sun 10–6 (last admission 5) 🚌 51B, 78A, 79 (Aston Quay); sightseeing buses to Kilmainham Gaol 🚉 Heuston Station; Suir Road (Luas) 💷 Moderate

KILMAINHAM GAOL: INSIDE INFO

Top tip Get the guide to shut you into one of the cells, to **taste the grim reality** of four narrow white walls.

Hidden gem Don't miss the **Five Devils of Kilmainham**, five snakes carved in stone above the entrance door. Chained by the neck and writhing helplessly, they symbolize the containment of evil.

One to miss The **audio-visual presentation** pales into insignificance in comparison to the rest of the tour. If pushed for time, give it a miss.

At Your Leisure

Dubliners opposed the construction of the 18th-century Custom House, fearing that it would be an eyesore

5 Custom House

This is Dublin's grandest building, a great domed Georgian masterpiece started in 1781 by English architect James Gandon (1743–1823) to replace the old customs point further up the River Liffey. It stretches its portico and long arcaded wings along the north bank of the river, just east of O'Connell Bridge. Republicans torched it in 1921. It is not open to the public, but is impressive from outside. Much the best view of the Custom House is from George's Quay across the river.

➕ 202 C4 ✉ Custom House Quay, Dublin 2
🚌 Cross-city buses 🚉 Tara Street Station (DART) 💶 Inexpensive

6 General Post Office (GPO)

This splendid Palladian building (1814–18) is almost all that was left of Dublin's late Georgian architecture after the developers got their hands on the city centre in the 1960s and 1970s. The GPO was the headquarters of the Irish Volunteers during the Easter Rising of 1916 (➤ 20) and it was from its steps that Pádraic Pearse read out the Proclamation of the Irish

Republic. In the intense shelling that followed (you can still see shrapnel scars on the columns), the GPO was gutted by fire. Reopened in 1929 after rebuilding, it became a potent symbol of Irish independence. Inside is a plaque recording the Proclamation, and a sculpture of the mythical hero Cuchulainn, a symbol of Irish heroism.

➕ 202 B4 ✉ O'Connell Street, Dublin 1
☎ 01 705 7000 🕐 Mon–Sat 8–8 🚌 Cross-city buses 🚉 Tara Street or Connolly (DART); Abbey Street (Luas) 💶 Free

7 Dublin Writers' Museum

A beautifully restored and refurbished house, 10 minutes' walk north of O'Connell Bridge, contains this excellent museum dedicated to some of Ireland's greatest writers. There are photographs, first editions, personal belongings, letters, rare books, and masses of memorabilia to satisfy your curiosity about Swift, Sheridan, Joyce, Shaw, Wilde, Yeats, Beckett, Brendan Behan and many others. The audio tour of the museum helps make sense of the links between the writers, their politics and the environment in which they lived.

➕ 202 B5 ✉ 18 Parnell Square North, Dublin 1
☎ 01 872 2077; www.writersmuseum.com
🕐 Jun–Aug Mon–Fri 10–6, Sat 10–5, Sun 11–5;

Sep–May Mon–Sat 10 5, Sun 11–5 🚌 10, 11, 11A, 11B, 13, 13A, 16, 16A, 19, 19A, 22, 22A, 36 🚈 Connolly Station (DART) 🎫 Moderate

8 Temple Bar

In the 1980s Temple Bar was a run-down area, due for demolition to make way for a bus station. These days it's Dublin's trendiest and most innovative quarter. This is definitely a place to stroll without a time limit. Young Dublin architects have twisted roof levels, inserted metal panels, and used glass and ceramics freely as they have renovated the old buildings. Street eateries and serious restaurants rub shoulders; so do street musicians and artists.

The heart of Temple Bar is Meeting House Square, often the venue for open-air performances. Around the square cluster the **Irish Film Institute** (tel: 01 679 5744; www.irishfilm.ie) and **Film Archive**, an arts centre, the **Gallery of Photography** (tel: 01 671 4654; www.galleryofphotography.ie), and **the Ark**, with children's workshops and activities (tel: 01 670 7788; www.ark.ie; advance booking advisable). Wander around the Saturday morning food market while Dubliners breakfast out in the open air.

If you're looking for live music gigs, try the Button Factory in Curved Street (tel: 01 670 9202; ww2.buttonfactory.ie). Cow's Lane Market is good for Irish-designed fashion and accessories from clothes to bags and jewellery to lingerie.

🚩 202 B3 ✉ Just south of Wellington and Aston Quays, on the south bank of the Liffey. Temple Bar Cultural Information Centre is at 12 East Essex Street, Dublin 2 ☎ 01 677 2255; www.templebar.ie 🕐 Summer Mon–Fri 9–5:30, Sat 10–6, Sun 12–3; winter Mon–Fri 9–5:30, Sat 10–5:30 🚌 Cross-city buses 🚈 Tara Street Station (DART)

The sumptuously furnished State Drawing Room at Dublin Castle

OFF THE BEATEN TRACK
St Stephen's Green, just south of Trinity College, is a popular place to hang out in the sunshine. If you walk on south down Harcourt Street, however, and turn left into Clonmel Street, you will discover the much more private, tranquil and uncrowded **Iveagh Gardens**. A beautiful green retreat dotted with fountains and mature trees, the gardens are a great place to escape from the rigours of city life.

9 Dublin Castle

Grand occasions such as the inauguration of the president and European summit meetings take place in Dublin Castle's splendid State Apartments. Some of the original Norman castle still exists, but much is fine 18th-century rebuilding. You can examine all this, along with the restored 19th-century Chapel Royal with its carved stone likenesses of British royalty outside and its elaborate woodwork and plaster-work within.

✚ 202 A3 ✉ Dame Street, Dublin 2 ☎ 01 645 8813; www.dublincastle.ie ❶ Mon–Fri 10–4:45, Sat–Sun 2–4:45 🚌 49, 56A, 77, 77A, 77B, 123 🚉 Tara Street (DART) ✋ Inexpensive

10 Chester Beatty Library and Gallery

This is one of the world's great private art collections, notable not for its size (though it contains more than 22,000 manuscripts, rare books and miniature paintings), but for its quality. Sir Alfred Chester Beatty (1875–1968), a Canadian millionaire who made his fortune through mining and came to live in Dublin in 1953, put together his collection over most of his long lifetime. The Japanese scrolls are particularly fine, dating from the early 17th to the late 19th centuries. Religious legends, tales of romance and scenes of battle are painted in meticulous detail across rolls of paper or silk up to 25m (82 feet) long. There are

Japanese prints of actors and tea drinkers and courtesans with oblique gazes and tiny mouths, and a whole clutch of delicately carved *netsuke*, or cord toggles. Other exotic curiosities include tiny snuff bottles in mother-of-pearl, jade and porcelain from China, and an Egyptian love poem written in 1160BC, the world's most important surviving example of ancient Egyptian poetry.

Pride of place goes to the library's collection of manuscripts. Some of these are astonishingly old and rare, including ancient copies of the Koran, richly gilded and tooled, and a medieval Iraqi treatise on engineering, artillery and astronomy. There are also some very early biblical fragments, such as a Gospel of St Luke and a Book of Revelations, both dating from the third century, and the Epistles of St Paul, written out in the second century, and portions of the Books of Numbers and Deuteronomy dating back to about AD150.

✚ 202 A3 ✉ The Clock Tower, Dublin Castle, Dublin 2 ☎ 01 407 0750; www.cbl.ie ❶ May–Sep Mon–Fri 10–5, Sat 11–5, Sun 1–5; Oct–Apr Tue–Fri 10–5, Sat 11–5, Sun 1–5 🚌 49, 56A, 77, 77A, 77B, 123 🚉 Tara Street (DART) ✋ Free

11 St Patrick's Cathedral

St Patrick's Cathedral is a dignified church, large and handsome, dating back to 1190, with a tower and spire soaring to 68m (223 feet). Inside you'll find the memorials to

FOR KIDS
Dublin Zoo (tel: 01 474 8900; www.dublinzoo.ie, open: daily 9:30–6 in summer; daily 9:30–4/4:30 in winter; admission: expensive), surrounded by the wide open spaces of Phoenix Park, is good of its kind. Across the road from Christ Church Cathedral, **Dublinia** is an interactive heritage centre that draws visitors into Viking and medieval Dublin, with life-size reconstructions of houses and streets (tel: 01 679 4611).

The interior of St Patrick's Cathedral

Dean Jonathan Swift (1667–1745), passionate social reformer and author of Gulliver's Travels (► 26), and his companion "Stella", real name Esther Johnson (1681–1728), with whom he had a long relationship.

The cathedral also contains some splendid tombs, notably the 17th-century monument to the Boyle family (of whome the scientist Robert Boyle was a member), and a collection of memorials to Irish soldiers killed in British Empire wars.

🕇 202 A2 ✉ St Patrick's Close, Dublin 8 ☎ 01 475 4817; www.stpatrickscathedral.ie 🕔 Mar–Oct daily 9–5:30; Nov–Feb Mon–Sat 9–5, Sun 9–3 🚌 49, 49A, 50, 54A, 56A

(Eden Quay), 65, 77, 77A 🚉 Pearse Station 🅿 Moderate

12 Guinness Storehouse

Ireland's favourite brew has travelled to more corners of the world than the Irish themselves, which is saying something, and the first thing many visitors to Ireland want to do is to taste it on its home soil. The next step is to visit this exhibition at the brewery itself, to discover just why the "black stuff" has such appeal. Housed in a former fermentation plant, the Storehouse tells the story of Arthur Guinness and his brewery, with displays about how Guinness is made, how it is transported worldwide, and its hugely popular and entertaining advertising campaigns. At the end of the tour you get a complimentary pint in the circular roof-top Gravity Bar, with floor-to-ceiling windows and spectacular views over Dublin.

🏠 202, off A3 ✉ St James's Gate, Dublin 8 ☎ 01 408 4800; www.guinness-storehouse.com ⏰ Daily 9:30–5 (till 7pm Jul–Aug) 🚌 51B, 78A (Aston Quay), 90 (Connolly Station), 123 (O'Connell and Dame streets) 🚉 Heuston (train/Luas) 💷 Expensive

🔢 Phoenix Park

Phoenix Park (main entrance about 1.5km/1 mile west of the city centre) is the largest walled city park in Europe, covering approximately 800 hectares (2,000 acres). This huge expanse of land, laid out in the mid-18th century, contains woods, lakes, hillocks, streams and gardens, set against the backdrop of the Wicklow Mountains. The Irish president lives here in a mansion, Áras an Uachtaráin. Here, too, are 17th-century Ashtown Castle, housing the Phoenix Park Visitor Centre, the American ambassador's residence, St Mary's Hospital, and Dublin Zoo – all swallowed up in the vastness of the park.

🏠 202, off A3 ✉ Main entrance on Parkgate Street, opposite Heuston Station ☎ Visitor centre 01 677 0095; www.phoenixpark.ie ⏰ Visitor centre: Apr–Sep daily 10–6; Oct–Mar daily 9:30–5:30 🚌 37, 38, 39 to Ashdown Gate; 10 to NCR Gate, 70 🚉 Heuston (Luas) 💷 Park: free. Visitor centre: free

🔢 Glasnevin Cemetery

Glasnevin Cemetery was opened in 1832 after Daniel O'Connell (▶ 16) campaigned for a place where people of all religions could be buried. Today, it's not only the largest cemetery in Ireland but is something of a national pantheon of Irishmen and women who have played an important part in the country's history and culture. You can take tours with a historian to visit the graves of politicians, rebels and writers, including the likes of O'Connell himself, Charles Stewart Parnell, Michael Collins, Éamon de Valera, James Larkin, Countess Markievicz and Brendan Behan. Tours last around 1.5 hours.

🏠 202 off A5 ✉ 11 Finglas Road ☎ 01 882 6500 ⏰ Daily 8–4.30; tours 2.30 🚌 13, 19, 19A, 40, 40a 💷 Moderate

Parnell's headstone, Glasnevin Cemetery

Further Afield

NORTH OF THE LIFFEY

It's becoming more fashionable than south of the river. Check out trendy Smithfield; try the markets in Moore Street (fruit, vegetables and backchat) and Mary's Lane (Saturday mornings; horses and hoarse traders); Blessington Street Basin Gardens in an old canal bed; and for a freaky thrill, a peek at the mummified bodies in the crypt of St Michan's Church on Church Street.

Outer Dublin

Riding the DART (➤ 35) is by far the best way to taste the many delights of outer Dublin, and gain enjoyable views along the waterfronts, the Liffey and the city centre.

St Anne's Park

This quiet park, 8km (5 miles) from the centre, is little visited by non-Dubliners. It is crossed by a number of footpaths; the best runs down through the park's extensive woodland, past follies and temples hidden away among the trees, to emerge beside the coast road with wide views out over North Bull Island to Howth Head.

🚩 201 E5 🚉 Killester or Harmonstown (DART)

James Joyce Tower

The Martello tower that overlooks the sea at Sandycove was featured by James Joyce in the opening sequence of *Ulysses*. Joyce lived in the tower for a month in 1904. Today it houses a collection of Joyce curios and memorabilia, along with photographs, books and a selection of letters. The oval tower itself, built early in the 19th century against the threat of a Napoleonic invasion, makes an atmospheric place to visit, and from the roof you can enjoy the same fine view as Buck Mulligan did in *Ulysses*.

🚩 201 E5 ✉ Sandycove Point, Sandycove
☎ 01 280 9265 🕓 Apr–Aug Tue–Sat 10–1, 2–5, Sun 2–6 🚉 Sandycove (DART)
💰 Moderate

Dalkey

This quiet little seaside town 14.5km (9 miles) from central Dublin, immortalized with mordant humour by Flann O'Brien in *The Dalkey Archive*, is not so much a resort as a well-heeled commuter haven with a tangle of narrow lanes and a pleasant "out-of-it-all" feel. The Heritage Centre is housed in Goat Castle, a fortified house which has wonderful views of the sea and mountains.

🚩 201 F5 🚉 Dalkey (DART)

Killiney

Killiney is a very exclusive place these days, the seaside refuge of rock stars, artists and other fashionable Dublin escapees. The best thing to do once you are tired of celebrity-spotting is to climb Killiney Hill and enjoy the splendid view out over Dublin Bay.

🚩 201 F5 🚉 Killiney (DART)

Bray

Bray is a jaded seaside resort, 24km (15 miles) from the centre, with good sands and a plethora of cheap and cheerful amusements. Take a windswept walk around Bray Head.

🚩 201 E5 🚉 Bray (DART)

ST VALENTINE'S SHRINE

Ever wondered if St Valentine really existed? He did, and was martyred in Rome on 14 February, AD269, for performing outlawed marriage ceremonies for young lovers. Strange to say, his remains are in Dublin, and can be viewed in a beautiful black and gold chest under an altar in Whitefriar Church at 56 Aungier Street.

oldest district, The Liberties. Francis Street especially is renowned. **The Powerscourt Townhouse Centre** (South William Street) has an antiques gallery selling mainly silver and china. Here, too, is the Crafts Council of Ireland's HQ Gallery. There are many antiques and jewellery shops in the same neighbourhood. Beautiful shawls, scarves and woven goods from the **Avoca Handweavers Mill** (County Wicklow) are sold at their shop on Suffolk Street.

MARKETS

At **Temple Bar Market** (Meeting House Square), the best of artisan foods are sold every Saturday. **Mother Redcap's**, a covered market on Back Lane (Christchurch, open: Fri–Sun 11–6) has all sorts for sale, much of it second-hand. At the **Tower Design Centre** (Pearse Street, tel: 01 677 5655) you can watch craftspeople at work and buy their work.

Where to...
Be Entertained

Listings covering theatre, cinema, live music, sporting events and festivals are carried in papers, *In Dublin* magazine (published every two weeks; www.indublin.ie) and *Events of the Week*, a free sheet available from pubs and guest houses. The *Irish Times* website (www.ireland.com) and **Dublin Tourism Centre at St Andrew's Church, Suffolk Street, Dublin 2** (tel: 01 605 7700) are also good sources of information.

FAMOUS PUBS

Spontaneous entertainment is provided by Dublin pubs: **Doheny and Nesbitt** (5 Lower Baggot Street, tel: 01 676 2945) is renowned for politician spotting, while **Toner's** (139 Lower Baggot Street) is a delight and is said to be the only pub W B Yeats ever entered. James Joyce is just one of the literary giants to have drunk at **The Duke** (9 Duke Street).

NIGHTLIFE

Pub Music

O'Donoghue's (15 Merrion Row, tel: 01 661 4303) is renowned, and there's traditional music and good food in Dublin's oldest pub, **The Brazen Head** (20 Lower Bridge Street, tel: 01 679 5186). **Jurys** (Ballsbridge, tel: 01 660 5000) hotels offer regular cabaret. Outside the city, **Johnnie Fox's** (Glencullen, tel: 01 295 5647) is equally famous for its seafood menus and Irish "Hooley Nights", while **Howth's Abbey Tavern** (tel: 01 839 0307) offers traditional Irish music. **Taylors Three Rock Bar** in Rathfarnham (tel: 01 494 2999) has Irish cabaret. A young crowd heads for Temple Bar and other venues featuring Irish and international artists, such as **The Village Bar** (26 Wexford Street, tel: 01 475 8555) and **Whelan's** (25 Wexford Street, tel: 01 478 0766).

Nightclubs

Happening bands swagger at the **Sugar Club** (Lower Leeson Street, tel: 01 678 7188), while exclusive **Lillie's Bordello** (Adam Court, Grafton Street, tel: 01 679 9204) is renowned as a haunt of the stars. The **Gaiety** (South King Street, tel: 01 677 1717) and **Olympia** (Dame Street) theatres have late-night music. For details of what's on at **The National Concert Hall** (Earlsfort Terrace) and **The Point**, see newspapers and listings. The **Comedy Cellar** (International Bar, Wicklow Street, tel: 01 677 9250) has comedy on every Wednesday.

Eastern Ireland

Getting Your Bearings

Eastern Ireland has subtle charms that well repay your time. The steep Wicklow Mountains rise right on the city's southern doorstep, and extend southwards with a fine coast of cliffs and long sandy beaches. South from here, big river estuaries (paradise for birdwatchers) cut into Ireland's southeastern foot around Wexford and Waterford. West of Dublin lie the great open spaces of The Curragh in County Kildare (prime horse country), while out to the north of the city the land smooths into green farming country.

Dotted throughout are the slow-paced towns and villages so characteristic of rural Ireland. Life runs as easy here as it does in the west, and with half the tourist crowds, even though the chief attractions of eastern Ireland are among the best known in the country. Dubliners may venture south from the city to take a stroll in the Wicklow Hills or buy knitwear from the weaving shops at Avoca, but many visitors look further west for their pleasures, hurrying through towards the dramatic scenery of Galway and Clare. All the more elbow room for those who allow themselves a few days to sample this overlooked corner of Ireland.

The hills of Wicklow offer superb walking and even better sightseeing, especially the monastic remains at Glendalough. Down in Waterford you can buy the world-renowned Waterford crystal glassware, while Kilkenny is surely the most appealing medieval town in Ireland. There are equine eccentricities at the National Stud and Horse Museum near Kildare, and a chance to see thoroughbreds at full gallop on The Curragh, Ireland's most prestigious race track. Relics of a glorious ecclesiastical past vary from the ancient churches

★ Don't Miss

❶ The Wicklow Mountains, Co Wicklow ➤ 76

❷ Rock of Cashel, Co Tipperary ➤ 79

❸ Kilkenny, Co Kilkenny ➤ 80

❹ Newgrange and Brú na Bóinne Irish Heritage Site, Co Meath ➤ 81

Page 71: The ancient church and graveyard at Glendalough

At Your Leisure

❺ The Wicklow Coast, Co Wicklow ➤ 85

❻ Wexford Wildfowl Reserve, Co Wexford ➤ 85

❼ Irish National Heritage Park, Co Wexford ➤ 85

❽ Waterford ➤ 85

❾ Jerpoint Abbey, Co. Kilkenny ➤ 86

❿ Dunmore Caves, Co Kilkenny ➤ 86

⓫ Moone and Castledermot High Crosses, Co Kildare ➤ 86

⓬ Irish National Stud, Irish Horse Museum and Japanese Gardens, Co Kildare ➤ 87

⓭ Hill of Tara, Co Meath ➤ 87

⓮ Battle of the Boyne Visitor Centre ➤ 88

⓯ Monasterboice ➤ 88

and round towers of Monasterboice and the Rock of Cashel to the carved high crosses at Moone and Castledermot.

Pride of place, though, has to be given to the remarkable Stone Age passage grave north of Dublin at Newgrange, heavily decorated with enigmatic stone swirls. One of Ireland's most memorable experiences is to creep along the ancient stone corridor to the chamber at the heart of the burial mound, where the sun still enters at the winter solstice as it has for 5,000 years. Nearby, the visitor centre in the restored 18th-century Oldbridge House is devoted to the Battle of the Boyne, which changed the course of Irish history in 1690.

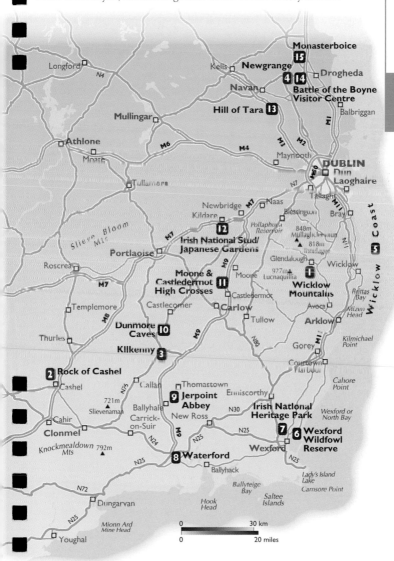

In Three Days

If you're not quite sure where to begin your travels, this itinerary recommends a practical and enjoyable journey around Eastern Ireland, taking in some of the best places to see using the Getting Your Bearings map on the previous page. For more information see the main entries.

Day 1

Morning
Leave Dublin (N81 or N11) in time to allow a morning's idling south through the **❶ Wicklow Mountains** (left, ➤ 76–77), leaving at least an hour to explore **Glendalough** (above). Aim to reach Avoca in time for a dip into Avoca Handweavers (➤ 92) before lunch in Fitzgerald's Pub.

Afternoon
Continue south via Arklow to Enniscorthy. If you have some time to spare, turn south here for half an hour to reach **❻ Wexford** and the **wildfowl** reserve on the mudflats of the North Slob (➤ 85). Otherwise, continue southwest to a night's stop in Waterford.

Day 2

Morning
Spend half an hour or so in the **8** **Waterford** Crystal Visitor Centre (➤ 85), then it's a 50km (30-mile) drive north to **3** **Kilkenny** (High Street above, ➤ 80), which is worth at least two hours' exploration and is a good place for lunch.

Afternoon
Take N76 south of Kilkenny, then R691 eastbound cross country to the **2** **Rock of Cashel**, where you can spend an hour or so exploring the ancient monastic site. From here, head north on M8 towards Portlaoise. Drive via Portarlington and Edenderry across the Bog of Allen, continuing to Trim, with its Norman castle beside the River Boyne, and on to Navan.

Day 3

Morning
Continue northeast to **4** **Brú na Bóinne** and **Newgrange** passage grave (➤ 81–84) – the site deserves at least a morning's exploration.

Afternoon
Enjoy lunch in the café at Oldbridge House, where you can also learn about the Battle of the Boyne at the **14** **Visitor Centre**. Afterwards, follow the N1 southwards back to Dublin; or if you are in no hurry, idle back via the rural and delightful R108 through Naul and Ballybogil.

① The Wicklow Mountains

The Wicklow Mountains beckon irresistibly on the south Dublin skyline, enticing city-dwellers out at weekends in their thousands to enjoy the fresh air and freedom of the "Garden of Ireland".

Roads from Dublin into the Wicklow Mountains are all beautiful. You can ease yourself in from Bray on the northeast coast, ride in grandly from the west via the Sally Gap or the Wicklow Gap, or wriggle down from the north over Powerscourt Mountain. The real pleasure of these mountains is in taking a side turning and discovering the beautiful gorges, glens and remote pieces of wild country for yourself. But the main attraction is undoubtedly Glendalough, a scatter of monastic remains along an exceptionally lovely lake valley in the heart of the mountains.

Filling the country south of the capital, the Wicklow Mountains rise in peaks that are small in comparison to the world's great mountain ranges; the highest, Lugnaquilla, rises to just 925m (3,035 feet), and most of the other summits struggle to make 850m (2,790 feet). But they provide wonderful walking, through a network of footpaths and along the long-distance Wicklow Way footpath, which traverses

The open country of the Wicklow Mountains

the range from north to south. Wicklow is the most thickly forested county in Ireland. There are excellent forest trails in the Devil's Glen on the east of the mountains, at Djouce Woods near Powerscourt, at Ballinafunshoge in Glenmalure south of Glendalough, and around Glendalough itself.

Glendalough

The monastic site of Glendalough incorporates a 12th-century **Round Tower** (33m/108 feet high), the 11th-century **St Kevin's Kitchen** (a beautiful stone-built oratory), and a number of glorious views of the lake and its mountain backdrop. Founded possibly as early as the sixth century, the monastery gained a Europe-wide reputation for learning. Its most illustrious member (some say its founder) was St Kevin, who was of the royal house of Leinster in the sixth century.

It is best to avoid Glendalough in high season: on summer holiday weekends, it becomes something less than the tranquil paradise it can seem on a quiet spring or autumn evening.

TAKING A BREAK

Stop in the Wicklow Mountains at the renowned **Roundwood Inn** (➤ 89), where excellent bar food is served in an informal environment. In Avoca, try **Fitzgerald's Pub** or the **Avoca Cafés and HQ** (➤ 89).

➕ 201 D4 ✉ Immediately south of Dublin, via N81, then R759 or R756. Alternatively, N11, then R755; or R783.

Tourist Information
🖳 County Wicklow Tourism, Rialto House, Fitzwilliam Square, Wicklow
☎ 0404 69117; www.visitwicklow.ie

AVOCA

The village of Avoca, in the Wicklow Mountains, was the setting for the popular 1990s TV series *Ballykissangel*. Avoca has Ireland's oldest hand-weaving mill. To get there, go 21km (13 miles) south from Glendalough on R755 and R752.

RESERVOIR ROAD

A scenic road curves around the shores of Poulaphouca Reservoir between Blessington and Hollywood – a good introduction to the Wicklow Mountains.

THE WICKLOW MOUNTAINS: INSIDE INFO

Top tips To get from **Dublin to Glendalough's** monuments and lakes, take the N81 Wexford road south from Dublin; at Hollywood (40km/25 miles), a left turn on to R756 takes you through the Wicklow Gap and on to Glendalough.
■ If you intend to go **walking in the Wicklow Mountains**, take a good map. The Irish OS 1:50,000 Sheets 56 and 62 maps cover the area in detail.

Hidden gem The **side road** that (almost) circumnavigates Trooperstown Hill, just east of Laragh and Glendalough, is a beautiful 14.5km (9-mile) meander.

❷ Rock of Cashel

As you approach the town, the outline of the Rock of Cashel rises out of the landscape, a medieval crown to a limestone outcrop. It was built as a centre of Christianity in the 12th century but for generations before that it was the inaugural site of the kings of Munster.

In the 10th century Brian Ború, later to become High King of Ireland, was crowned here; in the early 12th century his grandson gifted rock to the Church, although its Christian associations date back to the 5th century when Saint Patrick is said to have converted the king.

It's an exposed walk up the steep path from the car park, and as the wind whips around you on wintry days you feel relieved to get inside the heavy entrance door of the 15th-century castle. Visit the impressively restored Hall of

The Rock of Cashel, perched atop a rocky outcrop

the Vicars Choral up the steps to the right before going through the courtyard door. To the right you'll see a sign for the short film, and ahead a replica of the 12th-century St Patrick's Cross and the towering shell of the 13th-century cathedral, where highlights include the grave of former bishop Miler McGrath and Cormac's Chapel, which is closed while a roof is constructed to preserve the carved Romanesque figures inside.

Beyond the cathedral is the cemetery, particularly picturesque at sunset when the orange glows beyond sea of Celtic crosses and statues of the Virgin.

Painted wooden figure in the Vicars Choral

Cashel Town
If you have time, spend a few hours in Cashel itself, taking in the 13th-century ruins of Dominics Abbey, the Brú Ború centre that promotes Irish music and culture (tel 062 61122) and the Heritage Centre and Tourist Information office on Main Street (tel 062 61333), which has a model of 17th-century Cashel and sells traditional crafts.

TAKING A BREAK
Stop at Henry's Fine Foods on Main Street for a Panini, wrap or hot home-cooked lunches.

200 A3 Cashel, Co Tipperary 062 61437; www.heritageireland.ie Jun to mid-Sep daily 9–7; mid-Mar–May 9–5:30; mid-Sep to mid-Oct 9–5:30; mid-Oct to mid-Mar 9–4:30 Moderate

MILER MCGRATH
A controversial figure, Miler McGrath (c1523–1622) was both the Catholic Bishop of Down and Connor and the Protestant Bishop of Clogher, juggling his allegiances through the Reformation. Later he became Archbishop of Cashel. He had two wives, nine children (brought up as Catholics) and lived until the ripe age of 99 years, requesting to be buried in his Catholic bishop's robes.

❸ Kilkenny

Kilkenny is a medieval gem, ideal for a leisurely exploration on foot. War and wild times have swept regularly through the little town, leaving it with an impressive castle, a fortress of a cathedral, and a maze of sloping side streets packed with ancient buildings. Ask at the tourist office about Pat Tynan's one-hour walking tours, a quick and amusing introduction to the historic town.

Kilkenny Castle is a fine Victorian remodelling of the original 12th-century Norman fortress, superbly sited on a bend of the River Nore, with wide wooded parklands to stroll in.

St Canice's Cathedral

At the other end of the straggling High Street is **St Canice's Cathedral**, a squat 13th-century stronghold with a stubby tower rather like a head hunched between the high shoulders of the roofs. The nave is filled with beautifully carved old monuments and tomb slabs – a treasury of the stone-carver's art.

The Long Gallery in Kilkenny Castle

Climb the cathedral's round tower for the best view over Kilkenny; when you come back down, make for the little well house on Kenny's Well Road, just beyond the cathedral. **St Canice's Holy Well** here dates back to the sixth century AD – and probably much further.

✚ 200 C4

Tourist Information
✉ Shee Alms House, Rose Inn Street, Kilkenny ☎ 056 775 1500; www.discoverireland.com/kilkenny

Kilkenny Castle
✉ The Parade, Kilkenny ☎ 056 7721450 🕐 Apr–May, Sep daily 9:30–5:30; Jun–Aug daily 9–5:30, Oct–Feb daily 9:30–4:30. Guided tours only 💷 Moderate

St Canice's Cathedral
✉ Dean Street, Kilkenny ☎ 056 776 4971 🕐 Jun–Aug Mon–Sat 9–6, Sun 2–6; Apr–May, Sep Mon–Sat 10–1, 2–5, Sun 2–5; Oct–Mar Mon–Sat 10–1, 2–4, Sun 2–4 💷 Inexpensive

KILKENNY'S WITCH

The oldest inscribed slab in Kilkenny Cathedral is to Jose de Keteller, who died in 1280. He was probably the father of Dame Alice Kyteler, who was accused of being a witch. She escaped, leaving her maid to be burned at the stake in her place.

4 Newgrange and Brú na Bóinne Irish Heritage Site

Brú na Bóinne (Palace of the Boyne), a curve of quiet green farmland along a 15km (9-mile) stretch of the River Boyne, is the site of Europe's richest concentration of ancient monuments – henges, forts, enclosures, standing stones and a superb collection of neolithic passage graves: Dowth, Knowth and Newgrange.

Newgrange had already been standing for 500 years when pyramid-building first started in Egypt and had been in use for a thousand years when work began on Stonehenge. As you explore this mighty tomb of beautifully crafted stone slabs incised with mysterious carved patterns and symbols, your imagination cannot fail to be stirred.

The circular kerbstone wall and grass-topped roof of Newgrange passage grave

The introductory **exhibition** gives a good idea of the little that is known about the period 4000 to 3000BC, when enormous tombs like these were built all over Europe, and it provides an excellent introduction to the monuments of Brú na Bóinne, in particular the two great passage graves of Newgrange and Knowth.

The Building of Newgrange

Newgrange was built some time between 3300 and 2900BC, a giant mound 85m (279 feet) across and 15m (49 feet) high, its perimeter defined by nearly a hundred huge kerbstones. At least 200,000 tonnes of stone went into its construction, a mind-numbing amount of material to transport and put into position.

A passage 19m (62 feet) long, walled and roofed with more huge slabs, was built into the heart of the mound, opening out there into three chambers, like a shamrock leaf. It is thought to have taken the neolithic farming community between 40 and 80 years to build Newgrange – twice the life span of an active male in that hard and dangerous era.

The tomb sits high above the road, a great mound bounded by its circular kerbstone wall and topped by a green grassy dome of a roof. Outside the entrance (rebuilt since it was first rediscovered in a collapsed state in 1699) lies the Threshold Stone, a big weathered slab lying on its side, covered in spiral and diamond carvings. Above the doorway is a slit in the stonework like a large letterbox. It is through this unique roof box that the dawn light enters at the winter solstice.

The mighty, carved Threshold Stone and roof box at the entrance to Newgrange

Inside the Tomb

Once inside the tomb, the guide leads you by torchlight along the darkened passageway, sometimes stooping under the low stone slab roof. Spiral patterns are carved into the walls all around, well lit with electric light. At the end of the passage, you straighten up under a beehive domed roof to find yourself in the central burial chamber. The roof has survived intact and has rainproof qualities of which any modern builder would be proud. Vaulted with cleverly interlocked stone slabs, it has

The burial mound at Knowth is surrounded by other graves

kept the chamber perfectly dry for more than 5,000 years. The three recesses which open off this central area contain wide, shallow sandstone bowls, receptacles that once held the cremated remains of the dead

Riddles of the Tomb

If you lie prone on the floor of the furthest recess from the entrance, you can squint along the passage to see the roof box slit outlined in light.

On 21 December, the shortest day of the year – and for a couple of days each side – the dawn light creeps in through the slit and advances along the roof and through the central chamber until it reaches halfway up the back wall. Here it lingers for a few minutes, and then withdraws. As it is such a rare event, people wanting to witness this phenomenon need to enter their names into a lottery.

When Newgrange was excavated in the 1960s, the remains of only half a dozen bodies were found. Though speculation is rife, it appears that funerary remains must have been regularly removed from the chamber. Why remove them? Why labour so long and hard to build a device for trapping a momentary ray of winter sun? Did the ancients have a yearly midwinter clear-out of cremated remains, in the belief that the

Right: Characteristic whorls of 5,000-year-old stone carving at Newgrange

retreating ray of light had taken the spirits of the dead with it, perhaps to ensure the return of next year's spring sunshine? Or is there another explanation? Stand at the mysterious heart of Newgrange and your guess is as good as anyone's.

Knowth

Knowth, Newgrange's neighbouring tomb, lies surrounded by at least 17 smaller passage graves, like a cluster of big green anthills. The tomb has two passages pushing in from east and west, and is rich in spiral and line carvings. Whorls, zigzags and parallel lines decorate the great stones, offering powerful evidence that, like Newgrange, the tomb had a significance beyond that of a simple burial place. It was occupied for a much longer time than Newgrange was, however, from Neolithic times well into the Middle Ages.

A carved mace head, one of the archaeological finds at Knowth

TAKING A BREAK

Daly's of Donore (in the village of Donore, tel: 041 982 3252) is within walking distance of Newgrange and is open for breakfast from 7am to 10am, and for lunch from 12:30pm to 3pm.

➕ 197 D1 ⊠ Brú na Bóinne Visitor Centre, 11km (7 miles) southwest of Drogheda, Co Meath ☎ 041 988 0300; www.heritageireland.ie ⏰ Jun to mid-Sep daily 9–7; May and mid- to end Sep 9–6:30; Feb–Apr and Oct 9:30–5:30; Nov–Jan 9:30–5. Newgrange open all year round; Knowth open Easter–Oct (exterior only). Last tour of monuments 90 minutes before closing; last admission to visitor centre 45 minutes before closing
💷 Moderate

NEWGRANGE AND BRÚ NA BÓINNE: INSIDE INFO

Top tip Admission to Newgrange and Knowth is through the Visitor Centre; there is no direct access to the viewing areas. Visitors are taken to the monuments by shuttle bus. If you're visiting between June and September, it's advisable to arrive early in the morning and book your guided tour of Newgrange immediately. Better still, book well in advance. Those who turn up late in the day, unbooked, risk missing the tour.

Hidden gem When you are in the central chamber of Newgrange, inspect the **walls and roofs of the right-hand compartment.** They are richly carved with spirals and other motifs, well lit with electric light.

One to miss If hordes of visitors have descended on Newgrange, opt for the Knowth tomb visit – it's far less crowded, and the passage tomb art is better. But note that the tomb interior remains closed while excavations continue.

At Your Leisure

5 The Wicklow Coast

The Wicklow coast south of Bray and Greystones, the southern terminus of the DART (Dublin Area Rapid Transit) railway, is well worth exploring via R761, R750 and their side roads. Long sandy beaches fringe the coast as it approaches Wicklow on a long estuarine creek. South again are Wicklow Head, great for windy walks, and the Silver Strand around Brittas Bay, a fine strip of pale sand beaches. Arklow is an attractive little fishing town, noted for boat-building. The coast road makes an enjoyable return route to Dublin after a day in the Wicklow Hills.

✚ 201 E4

6 Wexford Wildfowl Reserve

Wexford is Ireland's prime bird-watching county, and the harbour of the North Slob – a tidal wetland just north of the town – is one of the best sites. About 10,000 Greenland white-fronted geese (one-third of the world population) overwinter here, along with many other goose and duck species. Swans, reed warblers, reed buntings, greenshank and redshank can be seen at other times of the year. The reserve offers well-placed hides (blinds) and guided tours.

✚ 201 D3 ✉ North Slob, Wexford ☎ 091 912 3129; www.wexfordwildfowlreserve.ie
🕙 Daily 0–6 💷 Free

7 Irish National Heritage Park

Allow a couple of hours for a stroll through Irish history beside the River Slaney, 5km (3 miles) north of Wexford. Reconstructed buildings range from pre-Christian round houses to a full-size *crannog* (stone defensive tower), a Viking shipyard constructing longboats, and a Norman motte-and-bailey castle.

✚ 201 D3 ✉ Ferrycarrig, Co Wexford
☎ 053 912 0733; www.inhp.com 🕙 May–Aug daily 9:30–5:30; Sep–Apr daily 9:30–5:30
💷 Moderate

TONELAGEE
The mountain called Tonelagee, one of the highest in the Wicklow Mountains at 818m (2,684 feet), seems to be presenting its posterior to the prevailing wind. Hence its name – which in Irish literally means "backside-to-the-wind".

8 Waterford Crystal

For over 200 years, Waterford was synonymous with its crystal, until it was bitten by the recession in 2009 and went into receivership, although the crystal continued to be produced in Germany and the Czech Republic. As we went to press, the tourist office excitedly reported that a new Visitor Centre is to open

Each piece is carefully inspected before it leaves the Waterford Crystal factory

in 2010 and craftspeople will be producing the crystal on a small scale onsite. Visitors will once again be able to follow the glassmaking process and buy Waterford Crystal made in Ireland.

➕ 200 C3 ✉ Waterford Tourist Information, The Granary, The Quay, Waterford City ☎ 051 875788

9 Jerpoint Abbey

The ruins of Jerpoint Abbey are worth the short detour south from Kilkenny. These beautiful buildings show work from several centuries between the Cistercian abbey's foundation in the late 12th century and its dissolution about 400 years later. Carved figures – one of a woman in a long pleated skirt, another of St Christopher with staff and upraised hand – stand between the double pillars of the fine cloister arches. A handsome pinnacled tower overlooks the roofless nave of the church. In the choir is the carved tomb of Abbot Felix O'Dulany, whose crosier is depicted being swallowed by a snake.

➕ 200 C3 ✉ Thomastown, Co Kilkenny ☎ 056 772 4623; www.heritageireland.ie ◉ Jun to mid-Sep daily 10–6; mid-Sep to Oct, Mar–May 10–5; Nov–Feb 10–4 💶 Inexpensive

10 Dunmore Caves

A guided tour takes you along walkways (with 106 steps) through this

The nave of Jerpoint Abbey's church with its Romanesque arches

series of well-lit limestone caves. The caves are of sombre repute: legend says that the Lord of the Mice was slain here, while a more credible story tells of hundreds of locals slaughtered in the caves by Vikings in AD928; skeletons of women and children have been found (though without signs of violence), along with Viking coins. You can see how the caves got their spooky reputation as you walk from one bizarre and freakish stalactite and stalagmite formation to the next.

➕ 200 C4 ✉ Mothel, near Castlecomer, Co Kilkenny ☎ 056 776 7726 ◉ Mar to mid-Jun, mid-Sep to Oct daily 9:30–5 (last admission 4); mid-Jun to mid-Sep 9:30–6:30 (last admission 5); Nov–Feb 9:30–5 (last admission 3); guided tours only 💶 Inexpensive

11 Moone and Castledermot High Crosses

The pre-Norman high crosses in the County Kildare villages of Moone and Castledermot are worth a detour. The cross at Moone is over 5m (16 feet) tall; the two at Castledermot stand near a beautiful little Romanesque doorway and a ruined round tower. All three crosses are granite and are carved with scenes from the Bible.

➕ 200 C4 ✉ Moone and Castledermot are on N9, south of Naas 💶 Free

12 Irish National Stud, Irish Horse Museum and Japanese Gardens

In 1902 rich and eccentric Scots brewery heir Colonel William Hall-Walker established the Irish National Stud on the southern outskirts of the town of Kildare. The colonel was fascinated by astrology and exotic religion. Stallions and mares were paired off according to the compatibility of their birth signs, their foals' progress was charted by horoscope, and the boxes in which they were accommodated had lantern skylights to allow entry of the influential rays of moon and stars.

The nearby grounds were laid out in 1906–10 as a Japanese garden, symbolising the life of a man through a journey to the Garden of Peace and Contentment by way of such obstacles and encouragements as the Hill of Learning, the Walk of Wisdom, the Hill of Ambition and the Bridge of Life.

Allow at least a couple of hours to visit the National Stud's stallions in their stalls and paddocks, view the Irish Horse Museum (which displays the skeleton of champion steeplechaser Arkle) and stroll the pathways of the Japanese Gardens.

🚉 200 C5 ✉ Tully, Co Kildare
☎ 045 522963/521617; www.irish-national-stud.ie 🕐 Mid-Feb to Christmas daily 9:30–5
💷 Expensive

13 Hill of Tara

This green hill, surrounded by earthworks, has been an important site since late Stone Age people built a passage tomb here. Its heyday of influence was during the first millennium AD as the main religious and political centre of Ireland, where kings and priests would gather every three years to make laws and settle quarrels. Tara features in many Irish myths and legends – and in more recent history too. Daniel O'Connell chose the Hill of Tara, symbol of Irish nationhood, as the venue for a "monster meeting" in 1843 to oppose the oppressive Corn Laws. And his instinct was justified when more than 100,000 people turned up (some say a million). This is a wonderful place to roam and enjoy the superb view.

🚉 197 D1 ✉ South of Navan, Co Meath
☎ 046 902 5903; www.heritageireland.ie
🕐 End May to mid-Sep daily 10–6
💷 Inexpensive

The twin Iron Age forts on the Hill of Tara seen from the air

14 Battle of the Boyne Visitor Centre

The Boyne Visitor Centre is located with the extensive grounds of the restored 18th-century Oldbridge House, built on the site of the Battle of the Boyne. This historic battle, which took place in July 1690 between the Protestant King William III – the victor – and his father-in-law, the Catholic King James II, changed the course of Irish history. The centre gives a blow-by-blow account of the events leading up to the battle, the principle characters involved and the tactics used by both sides. There are various artefacts and arms, paintings and a short film, as well as trails around the grounds, and a café overlooking the gardens.

✚ 197 D1 ✉ Oldbridge, Drogheda, Co Meath ☎ 041 980 9950; www.battleoftheboyne.ie or www.heritageireland.ie ⏰ May–Sep daily 10–6; Oct–Feb 9–5; Mar–Apr 9:30–5:30

15 Monasterboice

An astonishing variety of historic Christian monuments is crammed into this compact monastic site north of Drogheda: a leaning 10th-century

Musket firing display at the Battle of the Boyne Visitor Centre

round tower, ancient grave slabs, the ruined shells of two venerable churches, and – in pride of place – three wonderfully carved high crosses. Best of all is the South Cross or Cross of Muiredach, over 5m (16 feet) tall. Its carved panels include depictions of Eve tempting Adam, Cain murdering Abel, an Adoration of the Magi that seems to feature not three but four Wise Men, and a Judgement Day in which St Michael weighs the souls of the dead while the Devil tugs on the scales to gain more than his rightful share.

✚ 197 D1 ✉ Off N1, north of Drogheda, Co Louth ⏰ Daily ✋ Free

OFF THE BEATEN TRACK

Try the strand of Curracloe, not far north of Wexford, for a memorable sunrise walk along miles of empty sands with only seabirds for company.

Where to...
Eat and Drink

Prices
Expect to pay per person for a meal, excluding drinks and service
€ under €15   €€ €15–€30   €€€ over €30

WICKLOW MOUNTAINS

Avoca Cafés & HQ €
You'll find delicious home-cooked food here, based on organic and locally produced ingredients. Delicatessen foods include farmhouse cheeses, home-baked breads and preserves, and vegetarians do especially well. There are two eateries here, the self-service Sugar Tree Café with a veranda overlooking the garden, and the Fern House restaurant, styled like a Victorian fern house.
🕂 201 E5 ⊠ Kilmacanoge, Co Wicklow
☎ 01 286 7466; www.avoca.ie ⓦ Sugar

Tree Café: Mon–Fri 9–5, Sat 10–5, Sun 10–5:30. Fern House: Mon–Sat 9:30–5, Sun 9:30–6

Roundwood Inn €–€€€
The perfect place to take a break in the Wicklow Mountains, this renowned inn has everything: roaring log fires, excellent bar food and a formal restaurant (requiring reservations). Specialities include substantial soups, Galway oysters, smoked Wicklow trout and hearty hot meals including the house version of Irish stew.
🕂 201 D4 ⊠ Roundwood, Co Wicklow ☎ 01 281 8107 ⓦ Bar meals: daily 12:30–9:30.

Restaurant: Fri–Sat 7:30–midnight, Sun lunch from 1pm, 7:30–midnight

WATERFORD

Bodega! €€
There's a warm, wine-bar feel to Bodega!: keeping with its Spanish name, it has a distinctly Mediterranean atmosphere, and spicy notes in the fish stews and meaty dishes. There's a great choice of puddings to finish.
🕂 200 C3 ⊠ John Street, Waterford
☎ 051 844 77; www.bodegawaterford.com
ⓦ Mon–Wed 12–5, 5:30–10, Thu–Fri 12–5, 5:30–10:30, Sat 5:30–10:30

WATERFORD AREA

The Tannery €€€
The Tannery offers you bouillabaisse the way Maman used to make it, a lasagne of wild rabbit steaming with sage or you can go for a steak and kidney pie crust. Save space for a fantastic combination of sweet brie with

truffle honey and candied almonds. If you're impressed, you can even register for one of the courses and demos at the cookery school here, devised by the restaurant's chef founder, Paul Flynn.
🕂 200 B2 ⊠ 10, Quay Street, Dungarvan, Co Waterford ☎ 058 45420;
www.tannery.ie ⓦ Lunch Fri 12:30–2:30. Sun 12:30–3; dinner Tue–Sat 6–9:30

CASHEL

Cashel Palace Hotel €€
Built in 1730 as a bishop's residence, Cashel Palace is a beautifully proportioned Queen Anne-style house. The informal Bishop's Buttery restaurant in the basement is open all day, and the Guinness Bar serves light snacks from 12 noon until late. Some of the reception rooms and bedrooms overlook the gardens and have views of the Rock of Cashel.
🕂 200 A3 ⊠ Main Street, Cashel
☎ 062 62707; www.cashel-palace.ie
ⓦ Noon–late

Chez Hans €€–€€€

Occupying a 100-year-old former Wesleyan chapel under the Rock of Cashel, this restaurant keeps winning accolades. And justifiably so: its seasonal menus offer a wide choice and put local ingredients to the best use in classic French cooking. Specialities include fresh fish and shellfish, roast duckling and Tipperary lamb. There's always a good selection of farmhouse cheeses and an irresistible dessert tasting-plate.

✚ **200 A3** ☒ Moor Lane, Cashel, Co Tipperary ☎ 062 6117l; www.chezhans. net ◉ Tue–Sat 6:30–10; closed 3 weeks Jan

KILKENNY

Campagne €€–€€€

Opened in 2008, this contemporary restaurant has bright, funky paintings of country life lining its walls. But it's the modern French menu and Irish produce that has brought it much acclaim. Choose from mouth-watering plates of

gratin of veal, saddle of venison, sauteed scallops or roast hake.

✚ **200 C4** ☒ The Arches, 5 Gashouse Lane, Kilkenny ☎ 056 777 2858; www.campagne.ie ◉ Wed–Thu, Sat 6–10, Fri 12:30–2:30, 6–10, Sun 12:30–4

Langton's €€

In the Langton House Hotel, this is one of Kilkenny's better restaurants and a member of "the Kilkenny good food circle". You can enjoy an aperitif or a pint of Smithwicks at the shiny bar or head straight for the restaurant to feast on classic dishes such as steak, oven-baked salmon and roast duckling, plus some oriental-style cuisine.

✚ **200 C4** ☒ Langton House Hotel, 69 John Street, Kilkenny ☎ 056 776 5133; www.langtons.ie ◉ Mon–Sat 6–10:30, Sun 6–9:30

MOONE AREA

Ballymore Inn €€

Barry and Georgina O'Sullivan have recently renovated this country pub

into a stylish restaurant, complete with tiled floor and open fire. Here you can enjoy stone oven-baked sourdough pizzas or main courses of Irish ingredients like West Cork beef, Slaney lamb or Duncannon cod. Families often opt to eat from the smaller menu in the bright back bar with its TVs and contemporary paintings.

✚ **201 D5** ☒ Ballymore Eustace, Co Kildare ☎ 045 864585; www.ballymoreinn.com ◉ Restaurant: Tue–Thu 12:30–3, 6–9, Fri–Sat 12:30–9:30, Sun 12:30–7, Mon 12:30–3

Moone High Cross Inn €

This 1870s country pub near Kilkea Castle (▶ 91) has open fires in both bars. The larger bar serves traditional dishes such as a comprehensive Irish breakfast, Irish stew and bacon and cabbage. There are eight bedrooms with bathrooms upstairs.

✚ **200 C4** ☒ Bolton Hill, Moone, Co Kildare ☎ 059 862 4112 ◉ Mon–Thu 8am–11:30pm, Fri–Sat 8am–12:30am, Sun 8am–11pm

NEWGRANGE AREA

D'Vine Wine Bar & Restaurant €€

This small, red-fronted restaurant near Drogheda's old abbey serves a tasty Italian menu with a touch of French cuisine. Nibble away on Parma ham, olives and bruschetta, pasta and risotto, accompanied by a glass of carefully selected wine.

✚ **197 D1** ☒ 4 Patrickswell Lane, Drogheda, Co Louth ☎ 041 980 0440; www.dvine.ie ◉ Mon–Tue 12–3, Wed–Sat 12–3, 6–11

Forge Gallery Restaurant €€–€€€

This two-storey restaurant is furnished and decorated with flair, making a fine setting for the excellent food and service. Menus combine country French, New Irish and world cuisines, using seasonal and largely local ingredients.

✚ **197 D1** ☒ Collon, Co Louth ☎ 041 982 6272; www.forgegalleryrestaurant.ie ◉ Dinner: Tue–Sat 7–9:30; closed 1 week Jan and over Christmas

Where to...
Stay

Prices
Expect to pay per night for a double room
€ under €70   €€ €70–€130   €€€ over €130

WICKLOW MOUNTAINS

Ritz Carlton Powerscourt €€€

Splendidly arcaded in a modern twist on the Palladian style, the Ritz Carlton Powerscourt is sited in an estate whose centrepiece is one of the grandest 18th-century country houses and most superb gardens in the countryside around Dublin. If you are pushing the boat out for a special anniversary, this is absolutely the place to aim for. Service, setting and ambience are out of this world.

☦ **201 E5** ⊠ Enniskerry, Co Wicklow ☎ 01 274 8888; www.ritzcarlton.com

WATERFORD

Foxmount Country House €€

This 17th-century house is situated on a working dairy farm, just 15 minutes' drive from Waterford city centre. Yet it offers guests tranquility, comfort and delicious home-cooked food. There's table tennis and a hard tennis court, and the accommodation includes a family room; all bedrooms have private bathrooms.

☦ **200 C3** ⊠ Passage East Road, off Dunmore East Road, Waterford, Co Waterford ☎ 051 874308; www.foxmountcountryhouse. com ⊛ Closed Nov–Mar

Hanora's Cottage €€–€€€

Up in the mountains about an hours drive from Waterford, this hospitable, but child-free, guest house makes a perfect base for bird-watching, walking or horseback-riding. There is luxurious accommodation, legendary breakfasts and home-baked bread. The restaurant specializes in good local produce.

☦ **200 B3** ⊠ Nire Valley, Ballymacarbery, via Clonmel, Co Waterford ☎ 052 36134; www.hanorascottage.com ⊛ Restaurant closed Sun

KILKENNY

Rosquil House €€

This modern B&B provides spacious and comfortable accommodation within walking distance of Kilkenny's historic centre. Set back from the road, even the front guestrooms are peaceful at night, and the ample breakfast will set you up for the day. There are also self-catering units available.

☦ **200 C4** ⊠ Castlecomer Road, Kilkenny ☎ 056 772 1419; www.rosquilhouse.com

CASTLEDERMOT

Kilkea Castle & Golf Club €€€

This 12th-century castle is now a romantic hotel where many rooms have views over gardens, countryside and a golf course. The best bedrooms are in the castle; the rest surround an adjacent courtyard.

☦ **200 C4** ⊠ Castledermot, Co Kildare ☎ 059 914 5156; www.kilkeacastle.ie ⊛ Closed 24–26 Dec

NEWGRANGE AREA

Killyon Guesthouse €

Michael and Sheila Fogarty won two prestigious awards in 2007 – Georgina Campbell's Bed & Breakfast of the Year, and Irish Breakfast Awards: Best B&B Breakfast. That says it all for this delightful, warm and brilliantly run guesthouse.

☦ **197 D1** ⊠ Dublin Road, Navan, Co Meath ☎ 046 907 1224; www.killyonguesthouse.ie

Where to...
Shop

See the mill in operation at **Avoca Handweavers** (Kilmacanogue, tel: 01 274 6900). They sell fabrics, clothing, crafts and specialist foods. For country clothing try **Fishers of Newtownmountkennedy** (tel: 01 281 9404). Roundwood village has gift shops and a Sunday afternoon market. Distinctive pots are hand-thrown at the **Kiltrea Bridge Pottery** (Enniscorthy, County Wexford, tel: 053 923 5107).

KILKENNY

At **Kilkenny Design Centre** (tel: 056 772 2118), opposite the castle, there is the largest selection of crafts in Ireland, including textiles, ceramics and jewellery. Also look for the jewellery of family business **Murphy** (85 High Street, tel: 056

772 1127) and the books, toys and games at the child-friendly **Byrne's Kilkenny** book shop (82 High Street, tel: 056 772 3400).

BENNETTSBRIDGE AND THOMASTOWN

Visit the **Stoneware Jackson Studio** (Ballyreddin, tel: 056 772 7175), as well as the **Nicholas Mosse Pottery** (tel: 056 772 7505), renowned for traditional spongeware. At nearby Thomastown, watch lead crystal being hand-blown at the **Jerpoint Glass Studio** (tel: 056 772 4350).

TIMOLIN

Allow time to stop at the **Irish Pewter Mill** (tel: 059 862 4164) at Timolin, in County Kildare.

Where to...
Be Entertained

OUTDOOR ACTIVITIES

Options for outdoor activities in the Wicklow Mountains include walking, cycling, horseback riding, angling and golf. Local tourist information offices can provide details. There's also an **Adventure Centre** (tel: 01 458 2889) on the Blessington Lakes.

Horse Country

County Tipperary is home to three racecourses: Thurles, Clonmel and Tipperary. Kildare has three race-courses: The Curragh (tel: 045 441205), Punchestown (tel: 045 897704) and Naas (tel: 045 897391). Horseback-riding lessons are available at **Warrington Top Flight Equestrian Centre** (tel: 056 772 2682).

Golf

The Arnold Palmer-designed **K Club** (Straffan, County Kildare, tel: 01 601 7200) is a challenging course, and hosted the 2006 Ryder Cup. There's also **Kilkea Castle** (Castledermot, County Kildare, tel: 059 914156), set in rolling parkland.

MUSIC

You will find live traditional music all over the region on various nights of the week. In Waterford, **T and H Doolans** (George's Street, tel: 051 841504), has music on summer nights and winter weekends. The **Wexford Opera Festival** (tel: 053 22144) from mid-October to early November stages a selection of rarely performed operas.

Southwest
Ireland

Getting Your Bearings

The wild Atlantic blows up hundreds of storms a year along the coasts of counties Cork and Kerry, at the southwestern tip of Ireland. Here waves and wind have eaten away at the coast, creating big, ragged-edged peninsulas where the land faces directly into the Atlantic, and sheltered little coves between rocky headlands on the south-facing coast of Cork. You'll find literally hundreds of fine sandy beaches to enjoy along this, the most spectacular coastline in Ireland. But there are also plenty of attractive and enjoyable places inland, especially in the side valleys of the Shehy and Derrynasaggart mountains.

Sailing, diving, sea fishing and water sports of all kinds are big hereabouts. The climate, though often wet and windy, is notably mild and frost free, so there are a number of exotic gardens with plants and trees you would normally expect to find far nearer the equator. The Kerry Way offers superb long-distance walking through the hills, and there's good trout fishing in the lakes of the Iveragh Peninsula (whose circular Ring of Kerry must be Ireland's best-known scenic drive) and Killarney National Park, justly famed for its beauty. Inhabitants of Kerry and Cork are well known for their laid-back approach to life and for their elliptical wit.

Kilkee N67
Kilrush
Loop Head
Tarbert Glin
Kerry Head
Listowel
Rough Point
Abbeyfeale N21
Ceann Baile Dháith
Ballydavid Head
An Clochán
Cloghane
Tralee Bay
Tralee
357m Stacks Mts
N21
Camp Killelton
Castleisland
N21 N23
Dún Chaoin
Dunquin
4 **Corca Dhuibhne Dingle Peninsula**
An Daingean
Dingle
Killorglin
Castlemaine
N70
An Blascaod Mór
Great Blasket Island
Dingle Bay
Lough Caragh
N70
Killarney National Park
N22
Killarney
10 **9** **Muckross House**
Doulus Head
1041m
Carrauntoohil
840m
Mangerton Mtn
Derrynasaggart Mts
Valentia Island
Cahersiveen
3 **Ring of Kerry**
Portmagee
Sneem
N70
Kenmare
N71
Ceann Bhólais
Bolus Head
Sceilg Mhichíl
Skellig Michael
Kenmare
Cathair Dónall
Caherdaniel
Castlecove
Ardgroom
707m
Knockboy
Caha Mts
Glengarriff
Garinish Island
Castletown
Bearhaven
Dursey Island
West Cork
7
Bear Island
Bantry Bay
Sheep's Head
Durrus
Bantry
Ballydehob
Schull
Skibbereen
Mizen Head Signal Station **8**
Mizen Head
Baltimore
Sherkin Island
Coast
Oileán Cléire
Clear Island

0 ___ 30 km
0 ___ 20 miles

★ Don't Miss

At Your Leisure

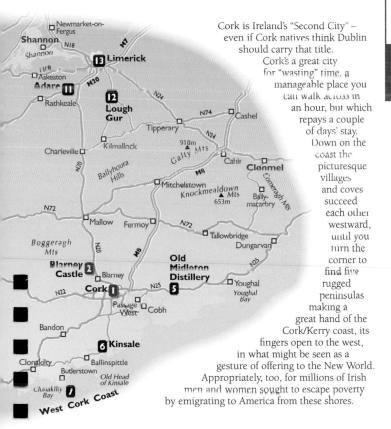

Cork is Ireland's "Second City" – even if Cork natives think Dublin should carry that title.

Cork's a great city for "wasting" time, a manageable place you can walk across in an hour, but which repays a couple of days' stay. Down on the coast the picturesque villages and coves succeed each other westward, until you turn the corner to find five rugged peninsulas making a great hand of the Cork/Kerry coast, its fingers open to the west, in what might be seen as a gesture of offering to the New World. Appropriately, too, for millions of Irish men and women sought to escape poverty by emigrating to America from these shores.

Page 93: Fishermen untangle fish from the net at Kinsale

In Four Days

If you're not quite sure where to begin your travels, this itinerary recommends a practical and enjoyable journey around Southwest Ireland, taking in some of the best places to see using the Getting Your Bearings map on the previous page. For more information see the main entries.

Day 1

Morning
Make sure to allow at least a morning for wandering around **1 Cork City** (a tribute to Rory Gallagher, left, ➤ 98–99), looking in at the art gallery, having a snack lunch in the English Market, maybe climbing the hill to ring the Bells of Shandon.

Afternoon
Go on, you have to do it… make the short trip out north to **2 Blarney Castle** (➤ 100), and kiss the Blarney Stone. Then it's back into Cork to try out your new gift of the gab in the **Hi-B** (➤ 99).

Day 2

Morning
Make an early start south to **6 Kinsale** (➤ 108) for breakfast or coffee. Then follow the rural road west to Clonakilty (R600). Continue to Rosscarbery, sidetracking from here via beautiful Glandore, Unionhall and Rineen to steep and attractive little Castletownshend. Then head west via Skibbereen to reach the one-time hippy hangout of Ballydehob in time for lunch.

Afternoon
Cruise two of the **7 Five Fingers** (➤ 109): go out to the cliffs of Mizen Head to visit the **8 Signal Station** (➤ 109) and back, then round the mountains and drink in the wonderful island views of the Beara Peninsula. You'll be tired, and satiated with beautiful landscapes, by the time you reach **Kenmare** for an overnight stop (➤ 116).

Day 3

Morning

From Kenmare you can enjoy a fairly late start to make up for yesterday. Drive at your ease over to ⑩ **Killarney** (➤ 110), and stop for a quick cup of coffee; then set out on the wonderful circuit of the ❸ **Ring of Kerry** (➤ 101–103). Lunch in the Blind Piper at Caherdaniel (tel: 066 947 5346).

Afternoon

Look around **Derrynane House** and grounds (➤ 101 102) – home of Daniel O'Connell, "The Liberator" – then complete your leisurely tour of the Ring of Kerry before pushing on from Killarney to stay overnight in Tralee.

Day 4

Morning

Take the whole day to explore the ❹ **Dingle Peninsula/Corca Dhuibhne** (Blasket Islands, below, ➤ 104–107). A ten o'clock start would put you in Dingle Town in time for a stroll before lunch.

Afternoon

Carry on around the peninsula via Dunquin (Dun Chaion) and Cloghane (An Clochán) – don't forget a windy saunter on the Magharees sandspit! Then return from Tralee to Cork.

❶ Cork City

Ireland's "second city" is a charming place that quickly slows you down to its easy pace. The River Lee divides into two channels as it flows through, forming an island of the city centre. Bridges are numerous, each with a fine riverfront view, making Cork an excellent place for a town stroll.

South of the South Channel, **St Fin Barre's Cathedral** on Bishop Street is worth a visit for its exterior statues, its fine collection of 19th-century stained glass, and the delicately coloured mosaic floor of the choir. Lift the choir seats to enjoy the handsome carvings of insects that decorate the misericords (and spare a thought for the weary choristers who perched on these ledges during long services).

In the city centre the covered **English Market** off Grand Parade is a lively mix of food, drink, book and craft stalls. Nearby in the Huguenot Quarter, an area of the city inhabited in the 18th century by French Protestant craftsmen fleeing religious persecution, you can stroll narrow pedestrian streets between small-scale old houses, shops, cafés and pubs, all chic and sleek. Head north towards the river to visit the excellent **Crawford Art Gallery** (tel: 021 490 7855, open: Mon–Sat 10–5) on Paul Street.

North of the river, climb the steep streets of Shandon to reach **St Anne's Church** (▶ Inside Info) and take time to look around the craft workshops in the adjacent **Cork Butter**

Below: St Fin Barre's Cathedral and South Gate Bridge over the River Lee

The western entrance to St Fin Barre's Cathedral

Museum (tel: 021 430 0600, open: Mar–Jun, Sep–Oct daily 10–5, Jul–Aug 10–6). Half an hour's stroll west brings you to the Sunday's Well area, where you can learn all about the misery of 19th-century prison conditions at the old **Cork City Gaol** (tel: 021 430 5022, open: Mar–Oct daily 9:30–6, Nov–Feb 10–5; admission moderate).

Emigrants' Stories

Housed in the old railway station at Cobh, southeast of Cork, is **The Queenstown Story** (tel: 021 481 3591; www.cobhheritage.com; open: May–Oct daily 9:30–6, Nov–Feb 9:30–5; closed 10 days over Christmas; admission moderate). Cobh, formerly known as Queenstown, was once a port of embarkation for the United States. This exhibition explores the pain of separation, hardship and danger suffered by the hundreds of thousands who, over the past two centuries, emigrated to America on the notorious "coffin ships". It is detailed, moving and inspiring.

TAKING A BREAK

Call in to the first-floor **Farmgate Restaurant** (➤ 114) for excellent pastries and a view of the market

🔢 199 E2

Tourist Information Office
✉ Grand Parade ☎ 021 425 5100; www.discoverireland.ie/southwest

CORK CITY: INSIDE INFO

Top tips Try ringing the bells at **St Anne's Church** on the Shandon side of town. You can "read" your tune off a crib card as you ring, or go at it freestyle.
■ At the Crawford Art Gallery, make straight for the **Gibson Galleries and the Irish Art Collection**, which is by far the most enjoyable part.

Hidden gem Tucked away above a chemist's shop opposite the General Post Office on Oliver Plunkett Street, the **Hi-B** (it stands for Hibernian Bar) is an entirely unspoiled pub, comfortable, a bit shabby and very friendly.

❷ Kissing the Blarney Stone

Blarney Castle is a notably rugged and romantic-looking 15th-century tower set in beautiful grounds full of pleasing grottoes, ancient yew trees and magic Druidic rocks half-hidden in greenery. None of this matters to the majority of visitors, who have come from all over the world for one thing only: to kiss the Blarney Stone.

One legend says that the Blarney Stone was the pillow used by Jacob when he had his dream of angels in the desert. Another holds that the slab is only half of a much bigger stone, and that the other half is the Stone of Destiny on which High Kings of Ireland, the Scottish (and then English) monarchs were crowned. The best-known legend, of course, says that anyone who can kiss the Blarney Stone will have the "gift of the gab" (eloquence) magically bestowed on them.

Blarney Castle was once the stronghold of the MacCarthy chieftains, the former kings of Munster

Reaching the Stone
The castle is extremely popular: come as early or late in the day as possible to avoid having to wait and head straight up the steps to the roof, where you will find the Blarney Stone built into the outer face of a gap in the battlements. You'll have to bend backwards and hang your head down (over a safety grille, and supported by one of the sturdy custodians) to kiss the stone. One word to the wise…empty your pockets before you kiss the Blarney Stone, or all your money will trickle out as you lean backwards.

🚩 199 D2 ⊠ Blarney Castle, Blarney, Co Cork ☎ 021 438 5252; www.blarneycastle.ie ④ Jun–Aug daily 9–7; May, Sep 9–6:30; Oct–Apr 9–dusk; closed 24–25 Dec
🖐 Moderate

❸ Ring of Kerry

The Ring of Kerry scenic route around the Iveragh Peninsula is the most popular drive in Ireland, and certainly one of the most beautiful, with wild boglands, wonderful coastal views and fine hill scenery.

Lough Leane is on the eastern side of the Ring of Kerry

Along the Peninsula's Northern Coast

Starting in Killarney, you skirt the north side of mountain-framed Lough Leane on your way west to **Killorglin**. This atmospheric small town is best known for the three-day Puck Fair in August, where there's drinking, dancing, livestock buying and selling – and a goat on a podium presiding over the whole affair. From Killorglin take the side road to Lough Caragh – this route introduces you to the boglands and puts you in the right frame of mind for wilder country ahead.

Back on the main road (N70), Glenbeigh is the first village you come to. Below on the coast lies **Rossbeigh Strand**, a pebbly beach with a 3km (2-mile) spit of dunes and a wonderful view of the Iveragh and Dingle peninsulas. A steep hill road brings you circling back to the main road, on which you continue southwest in beautiful scenery. Steep hillsides, patched with small fields and farms, rise through bracken and heather to sharp peaks nearly 800m (2,625 feet) high.

Near **Cahersiveen** you pass the smoking chimney of a peat-fired power station. On your left just before the bridge into the village are the ivy-covered ruins of the house where Daniel O'Connell was born. O'Connell (1775–1847) was one of the most important political figures in 19th-century Ireland: he earned his nickname, "The Liberator", leading impoverished Roman Catholics towards emancipation (► 16). In the village a right turn past the eccentric 19th-century Royal Irish Constabulary barracks (now a heritage centre) takes you along side roads to two remarkable stone forts: first **Cahergall**, then **Leacanabuaile** on its crag, with the remains of ninth-century beehive huts enclosed within an intact circular wall.

Another worthwhile side-track from Cahersiveen takes you further west to Portmagee and the causeway to Valentia Island. This is a beautiful, quiet spot, with wonderful subtropical gardens laid out on the north side at Glanleam by Sir Peter George Fitzgerald, 19th Knight of Kerry, in the 19th century, and some spectacular cliff views on the north and west. Boats leave **Portmagee** for trips to the **Skelligs**, craggy rocks several miles offshore with remarkable early Christian monastic remains.

The steep shapes of the Skelligs are framed by a cave on the shores of Valentia Island

The Southern Peninsula

There are glimpses of the Skelligs beyond Ballinskelligs Bay (Bá na Scealg) as you climb out of Waterville over Coomakista, and breathtaking views forward to the island-studded mouth of the Kenmare River. Down in Caherdaniel (Cathair Dónall) a side road leads to **Derrynane House** (tel: 066 947 5113, open: May–Sep daily 10:30–5:15; Apr, Oct–late Nov Wed–Sun 10:30–4:15; late Nov–Mar Sat–Sun 1–5; admission inexpensive). The house was inherited by Daniel O'Connell in 1825 and is full of mementoes, from the bowl in which he was baptised to the bed in which he died. In the grounds are beautiful gardens, an ancient ring fort and a Mass rock, where Catholics would gather to hear Mass during the 18th century, when the Penal Laws forbade its observance.

At Castlecove a side track leads north to **Staigue Fort**, Ireland's best-preserved prehistoric fort, a round stone tower in a spectacular location up a lonely valley. After this the road

View over the mountains and lakes near Killarney

reaches pretty little Sneem, and forks left at R568 for a wild mountain run back to Killarney.

TAKING A BREAK

Two excellent places to eat and drink in Caherdaniel are **The Blind Piper** and **Freddie's Bar**, on a side road to Derrynane.

🗺 198 C2

Tourist Information Office
✉ Beech Road, Killarney, Co Kerry ☎ 064 31633

RING OF KERRY: INSIDE INFO

Top tips If you have **limited time** and simply want to enjoy a four-hour drive amid beautiful scenery, stick to the main road circuit: N72 from Killarney to Killorglin, N70 from Killorglin to Kenmare, N71 from Kenmare to Killarney.

■ For **the best view of Lough Caragh**, fork left at O'Shea's shop in Caragh village ("Hotel Ard Na Sidhe" sign). In 1.5km (1 mile) turn left up a forestry track (wooden "Loch Cárthaí/Caragh Lake" sign) for 800m (875 yards) to reach a wide parking place with a wonderful high view over lake and mountains.

Hidden gem Anyone with an extra half-day to spare, and steady nerves on narrow hill roads, should try the side road that runs northeast up the **Inny Valley** from a turning 3km (2 miles) north of Waterville (An Coiréan). It climbs to the Ballaghisheen Pass (304m/997 feet) between the peaks of Knocknagapple and Knocknacusha, then dips over lonely bogland to Bealalaw Bridge, where you turn left for Lough Caragh and Killorglin.

4 Dingle Peninsula (Corca Dhuibhne)

This remote finger of unspoilt countryside, stretching 50km (31 miles) west of Tralee, is a magical place. It has mountains and a rugged coastline, sandy beaches, small towns of character and a remarkable concentration of prehistoric and early Christian monuments along with the Blasket Islands (Na Blascaodaí) scattered in the sea.

You leave Tralee along N86, passing the big white sails of the restored Blennerville windmill, and travel 13km (8 miles) west to the village of **Camp** with the Slieve Mish mountain range on your left. The waymarked Dingle Way long-distance footpath – a beautiful wild walk – runs on the slopes above the road. High above Camp stands the 835m (2,739-foot) mountain of **Caherconree**. From below you can just make out a stone wall near the summit that marks an ancient fort. Legend says that King Cu Roi MacDaire abducted Blathnaid, sweetheart of the hero Cuchulainn, and held her there. But Blathnaid sent a signal to her lover, whitening the waters of the River Finglas by pouring milk into its spring. Cuchulainn attacked the fort, killed the king, and rescued his lady.

At Camp Cross, take the mountain road over to **Inch** (Inse), on the peninsula's south coast. The view from here is one of Ireland's best; giant sandspits and whorled sandflats in Castlemaine Harbour, with Macgillycuddy's Reeks on the Iveragh Peninsula as a backdrop.

Boats in the harbour at Dingle

The tiny Gallarus Oratory dates from around AD800

HOG HOARD

Locals will tell you about the Spanish treasure ship that was wrecked in Tralee Bay. A golden pig was salvaged and buried in a triangular field nearby – so they say. It has never been unearthed.

The Southwest Tip

The south coast road goes on west, turning inland through **Annascaul** (Abhainn an Scáil) and leads back onto the N86. The South Pole Inn by the bridge was run during the early 1900s by Thomas Crean, one of Captain Scott's team on the ill-fated 1912 Antarctic expedition. Next along is **Dingle** (An Daingean), a small town on a circular bay where a playful dolphin is a frequent visitor. There's usually traditional music at The Small Bridge pub. Try Dingle pie: mutton pie with mutton broth poured over it, a local delicacy. Every year on 26 December the town goes mad, as fantastically dressed "Wren Boys" play rowdy tricks on each other and attempt to drink the pubs dry. In the past, participants in this event used to hunt and kill wrens (hence the name), which, custom held, had betrayed Christ.

Towards the western end of the peninsula along the R559 are **Ventry** (Ceann Trá) on its perfect scythe-shaped bay, **Mount Eagle** (Sliabh an Iolair) whose slopes are covered with the clochans (beehive huts) of early Christian hermits, and, facing the open Atlantic, little **Dunquin** (Dún Chaoin), where the 1970 film *Ryan's Daughter* was filmed.

Out in the sea lie the **Blasket Islands**, the main ones being Great Blasket, Inishvickillaun, Inishnabro and Inishtooskert.

THE SLOW TRAIN
Along the road between Tralee and Dingle (An Daingean) you may spot portions of trackbed and rusty old bridges. This is all that's left of the Tralee & Dingle Light Railway, one of the slowest and sleepiest rural branch railways in the world. Its working life lasted from 1891 to 1953. A short section between Tralee and Blennerville runs restored steam trains in the summer months.

Between 1928 and 1939, islanders Tomás O'Crohan, Peig Sayers and Maurice O'Sullivan produced literary masterpieces about life on Great Blasket, whose population of 120 spoke little or no English and lived simple, remote lives. You can buy copies locally of their books. A fisherman will probably run you out to Great Blasket if you want to wander through the writers' ruined village; the island was evacuated in 1953 when life became too hard. The sense of place and isolation can be overwhelming; it's an experience not to be missed, if you have the chance. If not, console yourself by reading about it in Dunquin's Blasket Centre on the mainland.

Back Along the South Coast

Start your journey back through Ballyferriter (Baile an Fheirtéaraigh), stopping to admire the tiny **Gallarus Oratory**. Just 1.5km (1 mile) away is **Kilmalkedar Church**, a fine 12th-century ruin with some notable stone carving. Side roads lead to **Ballydavid Head** (Ceann Baile Dháith) and some headspinning cliffs. On a clear day you can walk the waymarked **Saints' Road** over to little Cloghane (An Clochán) on the north coast; from here determined walkers can ascend

There are 3 miles (5km) of sandy beach near Inch

The colourful streets of Dingle are busier in August

the 953m (3,127-foot) **Mount Brandon** (Cnoc Bréanainn) to St Brendan's Oratory at the peak. Before setting course back to Tralee, do make sure to take a detour up the sandspit of the **Magharees**. The beaches here are just about the best you'll find anywhere.

TAKING A BREAK

In Dingle, try **Lord Baker's pub** (➤ 115), probably the town's oldest bar. At **The Tankard**, west of Tralee, sample some excellent seafood and enjoy unbeatable sea views.

Tourist Information Offices
✉ Ashe Memorial Hall, Tralee ➕ 198 C3 ☎ 066 712 1288 ⏰ All year
✉ Strand Street, Dingle ➕ 190 A3 ☎ 066 915 1188 ⏰ All year

DINGLE PENINSULA (CORCA DHUIBHNE): INSIDE INFO

Top tips If all you are looking for is a wonderful bathing beach and endless clean sand to run or walk on, look no further than the **sandy spit of the Magharees** that separates Brandon Bay and Tralee Bay on the north of the Dingle Peninsula, 24km (15 miles) west of Tralee.
■ In spite of the crowds, **August is a great month to be in Dingle (An Daingean)**. You can enjoy the Dingle Races, the Dingle Regatta and, best of all, the idiosyncratic Dingle Show, where locals gather to enjoy home-grown fun.

Hidden gem On a side road above N86, 3km (2 miles) east of Camp, is the ivy-smothered ruins of the village of **Killelton**, abandoned because of famine and emigration. Just off the path is a solid stone box with walls a metre thick, the remains of a church built in the seventh century by St Elton himself.

At Your Leisure

🖬 Old Midleton Distillery

Jameson's old whiskey distillery, in the market town of Midleton 16km (10 miles) east of Cork, has been converted into a visitor centre. In the original distillery buildings you can see the biggest copper still in the world, a great groaning waterwheel, enormous iron-bound vats to hold the mash, and a display of barrel-making in the cooperage, before enjoying a tot of hot or cold whiskey. On the far side of the yard wall the New Distillery steams away, producing 23 million bottles of the golden stuff each year and filling the air with the sweet, pervasive smell of malt and spirit.

🕂 199 E2 ✉ Midleton, Co Cork ☎ 021 461 3594; www.jamesonwhiskey.com/omd 🕙 Frequent tours Apr–Oct daily 10–5; Nov–Mar at 11:30, 1, 2:30, 4 💷 Expensive

🖬 Kinsale

A snug little fishing town with narrow, twisting streets and old stone houses, Kinsale, due south

Explore Kinsale on foot and then relax at one of its excellent fish restaurants

of Cork, is incredibly popular with visitors both for its charming appearance and for its position at the head of a narrow rocky harbour, the estuary of the Bandon River. The town bears the rather commercial title of "Gourmet Capital of Ireland", but it does have some excellent fish restaurants and an annual Gourmet Festival in October that draws the crowds.

Climb Compass Hill to the south of Kinsale to enjoy a panoramic view over the town and the estuary.

🕂 199 E1

Tourist Information Office
✉ Pier Road, Kinsale, Co Cork ☎ 021 477 2234; www.discoverireland.ie/southwest 🕙 Seasonal

🖬 The West Cork Coast

The Cork coast is spectacularly beautiful all the way west from

Kinsale. The cliffs of the Old Head of Kinsale are followed by a succession of sandy coves, rocky bays and headlands, with villages such as Courtmacsherry and Rosscarbery tucked in picturesquely at their heads. **Castletownshend**, with a waterfront castle at the foot of the steep village street, is particularly attractive. Under a big chunk of sandstone in the graveyard of St Barrahane's Church at Castletownshend lies Edith Somerville; alongside is the grave of her cousin Violet Martin. Under the joint *nom-de-plume* of Somerville & Ross, the cousins wrote several best sellers around the turn of the 20th century, including the hilarious and (later) successfully televised *Some Experiences of an Irish RM*.

At the fishing village of **Baltimore** is a pub named "The Algerian". Its name is a reminder of a disastrous day in June 1631 when Barbary pirates raided the town and took scores of locals off into slavery.

The medieval beacon, Lot's Wife, overlooks the bay near the village of Baltimore facing towards Sherkin Island

From Baltimore you can ride ferries out to Sherkin Island and Clear Island (Oiléan Cléire), Ireland's southernmost point, in the aptly named Roaringwater Bay. On the north side of the bay start the "**Five Fingers**", rugged peninsulas cut by the Atlantic out of the coastline. From Schull you drive down to the great cliffs of Mizen Head (► below), as far south as you can get on mainland Ireland; from Durrus you can reach the tip of the Sheep's Head peninsula, returning by a challengingly steep and twisty mountain road called the Goat's Path, with great views over Bantry Bay and its islands.

The **Ring of Beara** is a road circuit around the mountainous Beara Peninsula. Three island detours are worth making here: to see the subtropical gardens nurtured in the mild climate of **Garinish Island** off Glengarriff; to hilly **Bere Island** a little further west (both accessible by boat); and by an exhilarating cable-car crossing over a wild tide race to rocky and dramatic **Dursey Island**, which lies off the very tip of the peninsula. (For more information on the Iveragh and Dingle peninsulas ► 101 and 104.)
🕂 199 D1

🔢 Mizen Head Signal Station

Mizen Head is Ireland's most southwesterly point, on a spectacular stretch of rocky coastline with wonderful views. A short walk leads from the car park (but there are 99 steps to climb on the way back), and you'll see seabirds, wild flowers and seals – even whales occasionally surface offshore. On the headland, you can visit the signal station, established in 1931, see the various interesting displays about safety at sea, including a navigational aids' simulator and an automatic weather station, and tour the former light-keepers' quarters.
🕂 198 B1 ⊠ West of Goleen ☎ 028 35115; www.mizenhead.ie 🕐 Jun–Sep daily 10–6; mid-Mar to May and Oct 10:30–5; Nov to mid-Mar Sat–Sun 11–4 💷 Moderate

9 Muckross House, Abbey and Gardens

Muckross House is a handsome Victorian mansion built in Elizabethan style with high-pointed gables and tall chimneys; it contains an appealing folk museum of bygones. Nearby are three farms worked by traditional methods (great fun for children). The formal gardens are full of exotic trees and shrubs; rhododendrons and azaleas are a speciality, and there's a fine rock garden. The wider grounds of the park give plenty of scope for lakeside rambles or jaunting-car (two-wheeled carriage) rides.

North of the house, in a beautiful position, stand the impressive ruins of Muckross Abbey, established in 1340 but mostly dating to the mid-15th century. The most striking features are the cloisters and the big skeletal east window under the huge square tower.

At the heart of Killarney National Park, this is a very popular and often crowded destination.

198 C2 ✉ Muckross, near Killarney, Co Kerry ☎ 064 31440; www.muckross-house.ie ⏱ House and gardens: Jul–Aug 9–7; Sep–Jun daily 9–5.30. Farms: Jun–Aug daily 10–7; May 1–6; mid-Mar to May and Sep–Oct Sat–Sun, bank hols 1–6 💰 House/gardens: moderate. House/gardens/farm: expensive

10 Killarney National Park

While Killarney's lakes and mountains are famous for their beauty, Killarney town is infamous for its rampant commercialization. Sightseers, walkers and adventurers have been coming to the area for nearly 200 years, and things are well organized. You might consider paying the fairly high fee for a trip in a horse-drawn jaunting-car; the drivers, a smooth-talking breed known as "jarveys", know every nook and cranny. Otherwise, aim south of Killarney along the roads around **Lough Leane**, the centrepiece lake of the 10,125ha (25,008-acre) **Killarney National Park**. You can rent a boat to get to Innisfallen Island, or venture into the hills to view the Torc Cascade and ascend from the Middle to the Upper Lake.

The area around the lakes can become uncomfortably crowded in the holiday season. That's the time to put on your walking boots and follow the trails into the mountains – the well-marked Kerry Way, perhaps, or the high and lonely Old Road to Kenmare, an adventurous 16km (10-mile) trek through scenes of wild beauty.

Muckross House has magnificent gardens all year round

Pretty as a picture – thatched cottage at the neat estate village of Adare

🔶 198 C2

Tourist Information Office
📖 Beech Road, Killarney, Co Kerry
☎ 064 31633

🔟 Adare

Adare, 19km (12 miles) south of Limerick City, is one of Ireland's prettiest villages, with thatched stone cottages and a charming riverside position. It was laid out as an estate village during the 19th century by the lords of the manor, the Earls of Dunraven, and everything here is kept neat, tidy and easy on the eye.

Monastic communities settled around Adare, and their work can still be seen in several spots: the many-arched bridge, built in about 1400; the parish church, a former 13th-century friary church; an Austin friary of about 1315, with a Dunraven mausoleum in the cloisters; and in the grounds of Adare Manor, now a luxury hotel, the very evocative ruins of a 15th-century Franciscan friary.

The manor parklands stretch for miles; there is a medieval castle, rare trees and woodland walks. **Adare Castle** is accessible only on guided tours, which must be booked in advance at Adare Heritage Centre.

🔶 199 D3

Tourist Information Office
✉ Adare Heritage Centre, Main Street, Limerick; www.adareheritagecentre.ie
☎ 061 396666 ☎ Adare Castle: 061 396566
🕐 Adare Castle: Jun–Sep daily 10–5 📖 Adare Castle: inexpensive

🔢 Lough Gur

In quiet countryside 27km (17 miles) south of Limerick, this is one of Ireland's most extensive and best-displayed archaeological sites. An informative Interpretative Centre, built and thatched to look like neolithic huts, takes you through the 5,000 years that humans have been established here. There are

FOR KIDS
At West Cork Model Railway Village on Clonakilty Bay (open: daily 11–5; moderate) you can play among miniature houses and a railway.

OFF THE BEATEN TRACK
An hour's ride from Baltimore by ferry, Clear Island (Oileán Cléire) is Ireland's southernmost point. In spring and autumn the island becomes a birdwatcher's paradise with spectacular landfalls of migrating birds.

The scenery is just as impressive as the archaeology at Lough Gur

guided tours, or you can stroll at will around the site. There are stone circles (including the mighty 45m/148-foot diameter Grange circle), tombs, ring forts, a *crannog* or lake island fort, and the foundations of several huts.

➕ 199 E3 ✉ Bruff, Co Limerick ☎ 061 711200; www.shannonheritage.com ⏱ May–Sep daily 10–5 ✋ Moderate

🔞 Limerick

The Republic of Ireland's "third" city in terms of size, Limerick has in the past struggled with negative press, but the city centre is well worth a visit. The most interesting part is

Limerick's Hunt Museum is in the Old Customs House

the principally Georgian Newtown Pery area, instigated by Edmund Sexton Pery (➤ 175) in the 18th century. The Georgian House and the Limerick City Gallery of Art are located in this area, as well as the well-lit, pedestrian O'Connell Street. The city is also home to the prized Hunt Museum, which has an important collection of antiquities and artefacts, and medieval King John's Castle, just across the River Shannon on King's Island.

FIVE GLORIOUS WEST CORK VILLAGES

- Courtmacsherry ➕ 199 D1
- Rosscarbery ➕ 199 D1
- Glandore ➕ 198 C1
- Castletownshend ➕ 198 C1
- Ballydehob ➕ 198 C1

Where to...
Eat and Drink

Prices
Expect to pay per person for a meal, excluding drinks and service

€ under €15   €€ €15–€30   €€€ over €30

Fenns Quay Restaurant €€–€€€

Right in the heart of the city, next to the Courthouse, this popular restaurant has recently been extended and refurbished to provide bright, modern surroundings. Roast chump of Irish lamb with zingy Moroccan spices and tzatziki is a dinner menu favourite, and there's a wide choice of equally interesting meat, fish and vegetarian dishes, plus daytime snacks, sandwiches and breakfast items

⊕ 199 E2 ⊠ Shuares Street, Cork ☎ 021 427 9527; www.fennsquay.ie ◷ Mon–Sat 8am–late

Greenes Restaurant €€

Great flavour and attention to detail are the hallmarks at this modern restaurant in a large 18th-century warehouse. Menus have Mediterranean influences alongside Irish traditions. Stylish and relaxed, with coloured tables and fresh flowers to complement the zesty cooking, the restaurant's ambience appeals to all ages.

⊕ 199 E2 ⊠ 48 MacCurtain Street, Cork ☎ 021 455 2279; www.isaacs.ie ◷ Mon–Thu 6–10, Fri–Sat 6–10.30, Sun 12:30–3, 6–9:30

Jacques Restaurant €–€€

This popular restaurant is a dashing Mediterranean-toned bistro serving good, zesty international cooking. You might find risotto cakes with field mushrooms, Gubbeen pork with apple sauce, or herb-crusted rack of lamb. Set menus change daily, and the à la carte menu is seasonal. Early dinner (6–7pm) is good value.

⊕ 199 E2 ⊠ 9 Phoenix Street, Cork ☎ 021 42 7387; www.jacquesrestaurant.ie ◷ Mon–Sat 6–10

Zaks €€

Zaks exudes fashionable and understated glamour, its neutral tones enhanced by large mirrors, chandeliers and draped curtains. The menu is equally as relaxed, with easy dishes like the house's own recipe batter fish and chips alongside goat's cheese salad, Atlantic seafood chowder and French cut pork. They also serve breakfast, early bird menus and have regular dinner offers.

⊕ 199 E2 ⊠ 4 Marlboro Street, Cork ☎ 021 490 5692; www.zaksrestaurant.ie ◷ Daily 10am–late

Ballymaloe House €€€

Since 1964 Myrtle Allen and her family have led the movement for good regional and artisan foods that brought about the current culinary revival in Ireland. The atmosphere of this comfortable house remains unspoiled and, although the food reflects current trends towards global influences, it is not over-sophisticated. A food philosophy based on allowing finest quality ingredients to take centre stage is still crucial. Reservations are essential.

⊕ 199 E2 ⊠ Shanagarry, Midleton, Co Cork ☎ 021 465 2531; www.ballymaloe.ie ◷ Mon–Sat 1–2:30, 7–9.30, Sun 1–2:30

Blairs Inn €–€€

In a quiet, wooded setting just five minutes' drive from Blarney this delightful pub has a riverside garden for fine weather, and roaring open fires in winter. Good traditional food, based on local produce such as Kerry oak-smoked salmon or Dingle crab, is served both in the bar and in the restaurant. There's live music, too, on Sunday nights all year and Mondays from May to October.

198 E2 ⊠ Cloghroe, Blarney, Co Cork 🕿 021 438 1470; www.blairsinn.ie ⓒ Daily noon–midnight. Bar menu: 12:30–9:30

Farmgate €–€€

The shop at the front of this establishment is a showcase for local organic produce and home baking. In the café behind is an irresistible display of freshly baked savouries, cakes and pastries; in the evening it becomes a sophisticated restaurant. A daytime sister restaurant, Farmgate Café (tel: 021 427 8134), is at the English Market in Cork.

199 E2 ⊠ The Coolbawn, Midleton, Co Cork 🕿 021 4632771 ⓒ Mon–Wed 9–5, Thu–Sat 9–5, 6:30–9:30; closed 24 Dec–3 Jan

Longueville House and Presidents' Restaurant €€€

This elegant, supremely comfortable Georgian mansion is set on a hill overlooking the River Blackwater. The river, farm and garden supply fresh salmon, Longueville lamb and game, fresh fruit and vegetables. The cooking is among the finest in Ireland, inspired by the quality of seasonal local produce.

199 D2 ⊠ Mallow, Co Cork 🕿 022 47156; email: info@longuevillehouse.ie; www.longuevillehouse.ie ⓒ Bar lunch: daily 12:30–5. Restaurant: 6:30pm–9pm; closed Mon and Tue Nov–early Dec

WEST CORK COAST

Annie's Restaurant €€

This intimate and informal restaurant is well known for its wholesome food. Fresh, local fish, local duck, West Cork farmhouse cheeses and smoked foods feature on the simple but tasty menu. Breads, ice creams and desserts are all home-made, too.

198 C1 ⊠ Main Street, Ballydehob, Co Cork 🕿 028 37292 ⓒ Tue–Sat 6:30pm–10pm; closed 14 Oct–1 Dec

Crackpots Restaurant & Pottery €–€€

A good reputation with both locals and visitors, Crackpots offers (at very reasonable prices) unusual and beautifully cooked meals, with ethnic and European influences brought to bear on modern Irish and international cuisine. The menus vary according to season, and cater for all tastes with plenty of seafood. And if you like the tableware, you can buy that too, because it is made on the premises.

199 E1 ⊠ 3 Cork Street, Kinsale, Co Cork 🕿 021 477 2847; www.crackpots.ie ⓒ Mon–Sat 6:30pm–10pm, Sun 12:30–3

La Jolie Brise €

Overlooking the harbour, this cheerful, continental-style café serves good, inexpensive meals and moderately priced wines. Menus offer continental and full Irish breakfast, hot smoked salmon, fresh seafood, well-made pizzas (also to take out) and pastas, traditional mussels and chips, and chargrilled sirloin steaks. There's also spacious accommodation.

198 C1 ⊠ The Square, Baltimore, Co Cork 🕿 028 20600 ⓒ Daily 8am–11pm

Mary Ann's Bar and Restaurant €–€€

This delightful pub dates back to 1846, and renovations carried out by its current owners have respected its character. The highly regarded food includes specialities such as the platter of Castlehaven Bay shellfish and seafood and delicious home-baked brown bread, as well as steaks and roasts. Portions are generous, and local west Cork cheeses should not be missed.

198 C1 ⊠ Castletownshend, near Skibbereen, Co Cork 🕿 028 36146 ⓒ Bar meals: daily 12–2:30, 6–9. Restaurant meals: Tue–Sun 6–9; bar and restaurant closed Mon Nov–Mar, 3 weeks Jan, Good Fri and 25 Dec

O'Connor's Seafood Restaurant €€€

This light and airy family-run restaurant has been going for three generations. It serves up ultra-fresh seafood, with mussels collected daily, prawns served almost straight from the net and a live lobster and oyster tank in the restaurant.

🚹 198 C1 ☒ The Square, Bantry, Co Cork
☎ 027 50221; www.oconnorsseafood.com
🕒 Daily 12:15–3, 6–10 (Sun till 9)

KENMARE

Packie's €€€

This stylish but unpretentious restaurant has flowers on the bar, small tables and generosity of spirit. Known for its intuitive, creative cooking, Packie's produces intensely flavoured Irish-Mediterranean food, often involving local seafood. Familiar dishes are given an original twist and there's always local cheese to finish. The proprietors, the Foleys, also own Shelburne Lodge (▶116–117).

🚹 198 C2 ☒ Henry Street, Kenmare, Co Kerry ☎ 064 41508 🕒 Mon–Sat 6pm–13pm; closed mid-Jan to end Feb

The Purple Heather €€

Daytime sister restaurant to Packie's, this bar and informal restaurant serves good, simple, hearty food. Soups are home-made, bread is freshly baked, orange juice is freshly squeezed; and organic salads, omelettes and sandwiches are followed by comforting puddings. Choice is good, but nothing fancy.

🚹 198 C2 ☒ Henry Street, Kenmare, Co Kerry ☎ 064 41016 🕒 Mon–Sat 10:45–6

KILLARNEY AND THE RING OF KERRY

Aghadoe Heights Hotel & Spa €€€

Many are the awards and accolades earned by this superb hotel and spa, set in breathtaking scenery overlooking lakes and mountains. The dining room looks out on this stunning vista as well, providing a piquant sauce for fine dining in the classic style.

🚹 198 C2 ☒ Lakes of Killarney, Killarney ☎ 064 3 1766; www.aghadoeheights.com 🕒 Restaurant: Daily 6:30–9.30. Lounge and Bistro: summer only 10–9:30. Restaurant closed earl Dec to mid-Feb

Chapter Forty Restaurant €€–€€€

For a high-end dining treat without the expense, this fashionable restaurant is just the ticket. The menu is inspired by seasonal and locally sourced produce, including dishes like pan-fried duck, roast Kerry lamb and seabass with scallops.

🚹 198 C2 ☒ 40 New Street, Killarney, Co Kerry ☎ 064 667 1833; www.chapter40.ie 🕒 Mon–Sat 5–10

DINGLE PENINSULA (CORCA DHUIBHNE)

Lord Baker's €–€€

"Lord Baker" was the original owner of what is probably the oldest bar in the area. Bar food (maybe crab claws in garlic butter or chowder and home-baked bread) is served in front of the turf fire. A restaurant with a garden serves good food.

🚹 198 A3 ☒ Dingle, Co Kerry ☎ 066 915 1277; www.lordbakers.ie 🕒 Fri–Wed 12:30–2, 6–10

LIMERICK

Chocolat Restaurant €–€€

A smart, relaxed restaurant in the heart of Limerick, Chocolat caters equally for corporate lunches, afternoon teas or celebratory dinners, with a few quiet tables on the ground floor and a vast space underneath for larger parties. The fusion menu ranges surprisingly harmoniously from walnut and goat's cheese crostini with Clonakilty black pudding to fajitas, salt cod fish and elegant gourmet burgers.

🚹 199 E4 ☒ 109 O'Connell Street, Limerick ☎ 061 609709; www.chocolatrestaurant.ie 🕒 Mon–Sat 10am–10:30pm, Sun 12–10

Where to...
Stay

Prices
Expect to pay per night for a double room
€ under €70　€€ €70–€130　€€€ over €130

BANTRY

Mossie's €€
This delightful country house is on the south side of the Beara Peninsula overlooking Bantry Bay. A former Presbytery, it now offers luxurious rooms, paying great attention to style and comfort. There is a choice between the elegant French Room, the charming Annie's Room or the luxurious Russian Room, all individually furnished. Light lunches and teas are served on the lawns during the day and Mossie's Restaurant serves a fine dinner.

🕀 199 C1 ☒ Uluskser House, Adrigole, Beara, Co Cork ☎ 027 60606; www.mossiesrestaurant.com

CORK CITY

Garnish House €€
Decked with colourful windowboxes, this nice little guesthouse is only five minutes' walk from the city centre. It's also handy for the port and airport, and offers 24-hour reception facilities. Some rooms have a Jacuzzi, and there's an extensive breakfast menu to set you up for the day.

🕀 199 E2 ☒ 1 Aldergrove, Western Road, Cork ☎ 021 427 5111; www.garnish.ie

Hayfield Manor Hotel €€€
Although built in the mid-1990s, this attractive hotel in the university area, less than 2km (1 mile) from the city centre, has the feel of a large period house. It's set in large gardens, and amenities include a bar, an elegant restaurant and drawing room, both overlooking the garden, and a leisure centre for residents only. Spacious bedrooms are furnished to a high standard and have marbled bathrooms.

🕀 199 E2 ☒ Perrott Avenue, College Road, Cork ☎ 021 431 5900; www.hayfieldmanor.ie

Jurys Inn Cork €–€€
Like other Jurys Inns (▶ 39), this central, riverside hotel is conveniently located and provides comfort for a moderate price. There's no room service, but prices do include accommodation for up to four people. Rooms are well designed with good-quality furnishings and have phone, TV, tea and coffee facilities and full bathrooms.

🕀 199 E2 ☒ Western Road, Cork ☎ 021 425 2700; www.doylecollection.com

KINSALE

Trident Hotel €€–€€€
This 1960s waterfront building enjoys one of Kinsale's best locations. It's well run, hospitable and comfortable; bedrooms all have full bathrooms, and there are also two suites with private balconies, directly overlooking the harbour. As an added bonus, the food, in both the first-floor restaurant and the Wharf Tavern underneath it, is well above average hotel fare.

🕀 199 E1 ☒ World's End, Kinsale, Co Cork ☎ 021 477 4173; www.tridenthotel.com

KENMARE

Shelburne Lodge €€–€€€
This fine old stone house on the edge of Kenmare has been stylishly restored. There's an elegant drawing room and well-appointed dining room where delicious breakfasts

with home-baked bread and hot dishes are served. The comfortable bedrooms with bathrooms are decorated to a high standard. Guests can eat at Packie's (▶ 115), which is owned by the same proprietors.

➕ 198 C2 ☒ Killowen, Cork Road, Kenmare, Co Kerry ☎ 064 41013; www.shelburnelodge.com ⏱ Closed 1 Dec to mid-Mar

KILLARNEY

Killarney Park Hotel €€€

This luxurious modern hotel has a country-house look and an elegant atmosphere. Spacious bedrooms, tastefully decorated in countryside colours, have large, comfortable beds and lovely bathrooms. Guests can relax in the spa, enjoy relaxing beauty treatments and make the most of the golf academy nearby.

➕ 198 C2 ☒ Town Centre, Killarney, Co Kerry ☎ 064 35555; www.killarneyparkhotel.ie

DINGLE PENINSULA (CORCA DHUIBHNE)

The Brandon Hotel €€–€€€

Tralee's largest hotel has spacious public areas, and bedrooms equipped with direct-dial phone, radio and TV. Some rooms are small, but all have well-designed bathrooms. The hotel has a leisure centre and swimming pool, as well as a cocktail bar and restaurant.

➕ 198 C3 ☒ Princes Street, Tralee, Co Kerry ☎ 066 712 3333; www.brandonhotel.ie ⏱ Closed 23–28 Dec

Castlewood House €€–€€€

Located on the shores of Dingle Bay, this luxurious guesthouse has individually styled bedrooms and immaculate grounds. They are renowned for substantial breakfasts that include traditional Irish fare as well as kippers, pancakes and continental options.

➕ 198 A3 ☒ Castlewood House, Dingle, Co Kerry ☎ 066 915 2788; www.castlewooddingle.com

Heaton's €–€€

This guesthouse has a lovely location, right by the water with spectacular views across Dingle Bay. Cameron and Nuala Heaton are welcoming hosts, and the accommodation is exceptionally good – all rooms have bathrooms with power showers, and the mini-suites have Jacuzzis. Daughter Jackie has attracted some renown for her excellent à la carte breakfast menu, a long list which includes local smoked salmon, Irish cheeses, Dingle kippers, porridge with a topping of Drambuie, brown sugar and cream, as well as the usual breakfast fare. Bread, scones and preserves are all home-made.

➕ 198 A3 ☒ The Wood, Dingle, Co Kerry ☎ 066 915 2288; www.heatonsdingle.com ⏱ Closed 9–27 Dec

ADARE

Dunraven Arms Hotel €€€

Although it is now a large hotel, this 18th-century inn still has a relaxed country ambience. Bedrooms are beautifully furnished with antiques, and have dressing rooms and luxurious bathrooms. Amenities include an excellent new leisure centre, and the hotel is a popular base for sporting holidays. The restaurant and bar both serve high-quality Irish cuisine with a decent wine list.

➕ 199 D3 ☒ Adare, Co Limerick ☎ 061 396633; www.dunravenhotel.com

LIMERICK TOWN

No. 1 Pery Square €€€

This luxury boutique hotel is made up of immaculately restored late-Georgian houses. Choose from period-style or modern rooms overlooking the People's Park. There's also the Brasserie One restaurant serving modern Irish cuisine and the Irish Organic Spa in the basement for some well-deserved pampering.

➕ 199 E4 ☒ Pery Square, Limerick ☎ 061 402402; www.oneperysquare.com

Where to...
Shop

CORK

Find local produce at the **English Market**, off Patrick Street. Antiques are best around **Paul Street**. Shanagarry is home to **Ballymaloe Cookery School** (tel: 021 464 6785), and **Stephen Pearce Pottery and Emporium** (tel: 021 464 6807).

KINSALE

Visit **Kinsale Crystal** (Market Street, tel: 021 477 4493) for sparkling crystal, and **Kinsale Art Gallery** (Pier Head, tel: 021 477 3622) for superb art and crafts.

KENMARE

Kenmare lace is famous (Heritage Centre, tel: 064 41491): buy antique lace at **The White Room** (Henry Street, tel: 064 40600), rugs at **Avoca Handweavers** (Moll's Gap, tel: 064 34720) and clothing at **Geeskemaria Kenmare** (Shelbourne Street, tel: 064 41410).

KILLARNEY

Mucros Crafts & Gifts (National Park, tel: 064 31440) and **Bricin Craft Shop** (High Street, tel: 064 34902) both sell attractive, high-quality gifts.

DINGLE (AN DAINGEAN)

An Gailearai Beag (18 Main Street, tel: 066 915 2976) is a showcase craft gallery. **Louis Mulcahy's** sells his pottery at a factory shop near Dingle (tel: 066 915 6229).

Where to...
Be Entertained

OUTDOOR ACTIVITIES

Activities include sailing (Castlepark Marina, Kinsale, tel: 021 477 4959), sea angling, cycling, horseback riding and golf; information from tourist offices. Kenmare's **Seafari** (The Pier, tel: 064 42059; www.seafariireland.com) makes an entertaining wildlife cruise on Kenmare Bay. Dingle is a base for dolphin-watching (boats depart regularly from the harbour).

SPECTATOR SPORTS

Greyhound racing (Curraheen Park in Bishopstown, tel: 021 454095) and horse racing (Mallow, tel: 022 502207) are popular. Also look out for the interesting local sport of road bowling.

MUSIC

Pubs in every town have live music most nights in summer. Good venues include: in Kinsale, **The Spaniard** (Scilly, tel: 021 477 2436); in Bantry, **The Anchor Bar** (tel: 027 50012); in Kenmare, **The Coachman's** (Henry Street, tel: 064 41311); and in Killarney, **The Danny Man Inn** (Eviston House Hotel, New Street, tel: 064 31640). Dingle is *the* place for live music, especially **An Droichead Beag** (tel: 066 915 1723) – but almost any bar will be humming. Contrasting musical treats are the **Guinness Cork Jazz Festival**, late October (www.guinnessjazzfestival.ie) and the **West Cork Chamber Music Festival** (Bantry House, tel: 027 52788) late June to July.

West and Northwest Ireland

Getting Your Bearings

The west of Ireland may not have as dense a profusion of dramatic mountains and wild peninsulas as the southwest, but it has something else – sheer magic.

A succession of remarkable landscapes blends one into another, each entirely distinctive but only a part of the whole captivating jigsaw. They include the naked grey limestone hills of the Burren in County Clare, beautiful with carpets of wild flowers in spring and summer; the Connemara district of County Galway, with its remote mountainous heart and harshly lonely coasts; and the three windswept Aran Islands (Oileáin Árann) in Galway Bay, where life and work go on at an

Carndonagh
Moville *Inishowen Head*
16
Inishowen
Buncrana

unhurried pace among the tiny, rocky fields and innumerable
stone walls. The countryside round Clew Bay in County
Mayo combines gentle green hills and forbidding mountains
with ancient field monuments. Dominating the whole area is
Croagh Patrick, the Holy Mountain. Then there's County Sligo
"Yeats Country" – and Donegal, a ragged-edged sea county
with truly wild hills and cliffs, where people are few and far
between.

This is the land that inspired playwright J M Synge and
novelist Liam O'Flaherty, painter Jack Yeats and his brother,
the poet W B Yeats. The landscape still inspires musicians,
some of the best traditional music is played in the West of
Ireland, from Clare's gently flowing tunes to the spiky reels
of Donegal. Here in the West you can play the tourist – for
instance at County Clare's Bunratty Folk Park; or you can take
the other road and savour the lonely silences of the Nephin
Beg Mountains. Whatever you do, be sure to climb Croagh
Patrick: you will never forget the view from the summit.

**Right: Fishing
boats moored
at Leenane,
County Galway,
on the deep
water of Killary
Harbour**

**Page 119: The
view across
Galway Bay**

In Five Days

If you're not quite sure where to begin your travels, this itinerary recommends a practical and enjoyable five days in West and Northwest Ireland, taking in some of the best places to see using the Getting Your Bearings map on the previous page. For more information see the main entries.

Day 1

Morning
Spend the day exploring the **❶ Burren** (➤ 124–127). Travel the slow coast road from Ballyvaughan down to **Doolin**, stopping at one of its famous pubs for lunch (➤ 127).

Afternoon
Carry on a few miles down the coast to the spectacular **❶ Cliffs of Moher** (➤ 126). Then take your time circling back inland by way of the great ancient monuments of **Poulnabrone portal dolmen** (above) and **Gleninsheen wedge tomb**, making time for a stroll on the Burren's naked limestone hills. An hour's drive in the early evening will land you in Galway for the night.

Day 2

Morning
Take the ferry from the city quays and cruise down Galway Bay to **❷ Inishmore/Inis Móir** (left, ➤ 129), the biggest of the Aran Islands (Oileáin Árann). Stop for lunch at Joe Watty's friendly pub in the small port of Kilronan. While in Kilronan, take a quick look at the Aran Heritage Centre.

Afternoon
Make your way up to the ancient fort of **❷ Dunaengus** (➤ 129) on the cliffs, preferably on foot or by rented bicycle. Be sure to be back in Kilronan in good time for the last ferry back to Galway!

Day 3

Morning
You'll have plenty of time for coffee, a stroll and a look around ⑨ **Galway City** (➤ 135) before moving on in the early afternoon.

Afternoon
Take the ❸ **Connemara** coast road west, at first along the smooth upper shore of Galway Bay, then winding in and out around a succession of small, craggy bays. After a cup of tea in **Clifden** (➤ 130), push on 65km (40 miles) by way of dramatic Killary Harbour to ❹ **Westport** (➤ 132). Stay overnight here, and look for a great music session in Molloy's (➤ 133), Hoban's or McHale's.

Day 4

Morning
Set off bright and early for the hour's run (via the bridge) out to ❹ **Achill Island** (coast at Dooagh above, ➤ 133). Back on the mainland, continue north on the wild coastal road to Bangor Erris, then turn east across the bleakly impressive Bellacorick bog to reach civilization and a late lunch at Ballina, perhaps at The Broken Jug pub (tel. 096 72379).

Afternoon
Push on to ⓭ **Sligo** (➤ 137; a pint in Hargadon's bar is obligatory here), and drive north towards W B Yeats's favourite mountains to pay your respects at his grave in **Drumcliff churchyard** (➤ 179). Then return through Sligo and drive on south for Galway.

Day 5

If you have a day for a bleakly beautiful corner of Ireland (right), stay overnight in Ballybofey and spend the next day driving the spectacular circuit of southwest Donegal's coast, out by Glencolumbkille (Gleann Cholm Cille) and the Slieve League (Sliabh Liag) cliffs (➤ 138).

❶ The Burren and the Cliffs of Moher

The Burren is 1,300sq km (507sq miles) of hilly ground in the northwest corner of Clare, almost waterless, all but deserted, and largely made up of naked grey limestone. Yet in this bleak setting you'll find superb wild flowers, marvellous music, hundreds of ancient monuments and a beautiful coastline, culminating in the mighty Cliffs of Moher. And with it all comes that special laid-back County Clare atmosphere. The place is a paradox, but one you'll have unbeatable pleasure in exploring.

A Snapshot Tour

Start in **Ballyvaughan**, following the coast road down to **Doolin**, noted for its traditional music pubs, and on to the **Cliffs of Moher** for some spectacular views. Then take the road for **Lisdoonvarna** and **Kilfenora**, and on by **Corofin**, to enjoy some typical laid-back Burren villages. There are carved high crosses at Kilfenora, and the excellent **Burren Display Centre** there fills you in on the geology and flora of the region. See more early Christian remains at **Dysert O'Dea** south of Corofin, then meander north through the heart of the Burren to find the magical landscape of **Mullaghmore**, the great portal dolmen of **Poulnabrone**, and, in spring and summer, the carpets of wild flowers.

You could see the "Best of the Burren" in a long day like this. But you won't begin to see the place itself until you leave the car and walk out into the wilderness.

The Cliffs of Moher make a great spot to view dramatic weather approaching

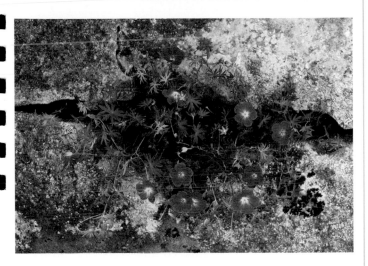

Wild flowers take advantage of natural crevices in the limestone

Floral Present and Stony Past

You don't have to be a botanist to see the beauty of the flowers of the Burren. The limestone pavements carry deep cracks, known as "grykes" to geologists. These trap water, sun and soil fragments making them ideal hothouses for plants. The warm Gulf Stream moves offshore; sunlight bounces off the naked stone into the grykes. Whatever combination of factors makes it happen, the Burren bursts open each spring with an astonishing array of wild flowers: orchids, spring gentians, mountain avens, eyebright, bloody cranesbill. Plants that wouldn't normally be found anywhere near each other grow side by side – acid-loving and lime-loving, arctic, mountain, coastal, Mediterranean. The ferns, mosses and lichens are spectacular. Springtime and summer in the Burren are a botanist's dream, and beautiful for anyone who loves colour and variety in the landscape.

Scattered across this landscape are monuments bearing witness to five millennia of human habitation. Around 5,000 years ago, a forgotten people built the **Poulnabrone portal dolmen** – the stone uprights and cap stone of which would once have been covered with earth to form a tomb chamber. **Gleninsheen**, near Caherconnell, and other wedge-shaped tombs nearby date from about 1500BC. With the introduction of Christianity came the wonderfully carved high crosses at **Kilfenora**, and in the 12th and 13th centuries respectively the monastic site of **Dysert O'Dea** in the south and the rich stonework at **Corcomroe Abbey** in the north. Round stone forts and enclosures with jaw-breaking names dot the hills: Cahermacnaghten, Caherballykinvarga, Cahercommaun. Under the hills stand fortified towers like the gaunt 16th century **Newtown Castle** near Ballyvaughan, and imposing houses such as the picturesquely ruined 17th-century **Leamaneh Castle** outside Corofin. There are also the shells of ancient churches abandoned after Oliver Cromwell's troops invaded and subdued the Burren in the 1650s.

Fine Scenery and a Good Time

A great way to see the Burren is to spend a couple of days walking the **Burren Way**, a 45km (28-mile) footpath from Ballyvaughan to Liscannor. The most spectacular part is undoubtedly along the edges of the **Cliffs of Moher** at the southwestern extremity of the Burren. At their highest point these giant flagstone cliffs fall sheer into the sea: a great tourist attraction, and often a crowded one. There are more tremendous views from **Corkscrew Hill**, a section of N67 south of Ballyvaughan that snakes back and forth as it climbs, and the whole of the steep, craggy coastline around Black Head.

ARCHAEOLOGY
Five of the Burren's great archaeological delights:
- Poulnabrone portal dolmen
- High crosses at Kilfenora Cathedral
- Newtown Castle tower house
- Dysert O'Dea's church doorway with its carvings
- Corcomroe Abbey

You can tour the underground **showcaves at Aillwee** near Ballyvaughan, and escape other tourists at **Mullaghmore**, a magical hill reached by a country road north of Corofin, to enjoy strange land formations and delicious solitude.

The Poulnabrone portal dolmen is impressive when you get up close

Spring gentian in flower near the Burren

FLOWERS

Don't forget your flower book! Mary Angela Keane's *The Burren* (an Irish Heritage Series paperback that is widely available locally) gives an excellent introduction to the Burren flora. Real enthusiasts should bring a hand lens with them for a close-up view. But remember – don't pick them!

TAKING A BREAK

In Kilfenora, try **Vaughan's** or **Linnane's**, and in Lisdoonvarna, the **Roadside Tavern**: you're guaranteed conversation and laughter. If you fancy a singalong in Doolin, **O'Connor's** is a good bet. If your taste is for traditional tunes and you're staying in Doolin overnight, try **McGann's** at around 10pm.

Tourist Information Centres
✉ Arthur's Row, Ennis and Cliffs of Moher; www.discoverireland.ie/shannon
☎ Ennis: 065 682 8366. Cliffs of Moher: www.discoverireland.ie/shannon

Burren Display Centre
✚ 199 D5 ☎ 065 708 8030; www.theburrencentre.ie
🕐 Jun–Aug daily 9:30–5:30; Mar–May, Sep–Oct daily 10–5 💷 Moderate

Aillwee Caves
✚ 199 D5 ☎ 065 707 7036 🕐 Tours only daily from 10am; last tour 5:30 (Jul, Aug 6pm); Dec by appointment only 💷 Expensive

---

THE BURREN: INSIDE INFO

Top tips Five of the **Burren's chief tourist attractions** lie on or very near N67: Ballyvaughan, Newtown Castle, Aillwee Caves, Corkscrew Hill, and the spa town of Lisdoonvarna. The Cliffs of Moher are 10km (6 miles) along R478.
■ Anyone with enough skill not to spoil the tune is welcome to join a pub **music session**. Don't be shy, ask if you can join in!

Hidden gems Holy wells, rock chairs that cure backache, Mass rocks and forgotten church ruins: the Burren is packed with them, and you can find almost all of them with the help of **Tim Robinson's wonderful Folding Landscape.**

One to miss Don't bother with the **Cliffs of Moher on a high-season weekend** – the clifftops will be crowded, and all sense of awe will be on hold.

② The Aran Islands (Oileáin Árann)

Seeming to float in the mouth of Galway Bay like three low grey boats, the Aran Islands (Oileáin Árann) resemble no other part of Ireland. Here Irish is still spoken everyday, the traditional black hide-covered boats called *currachs* are used for fishing (though now they're canvas covered and often motorised), transport is mostly on foot or bicycle, homespun clothing is still worn by some of the older folk, and the pace of life is driven not so much by the clock as by the tides and winds, and by tasks done and not done.

The islands are made not of Galway granite but of Clare limestone, which means that their spring and summer flower displays are glorious. Countless thousands of stone walls march in parallel lines across the bare grey and black rock, squaring off the islands into hundreds of tiny fields. Partly these walls show ownership; partly they are built of necessity, as handy repositories for stones picked laboriously from the fields by hand. The soil of the islands has been created by hand, a precious mixture of sand, seaweed and dung that grows the best potatoes in Ireland.

Inisheer and Inishmaan

Inisheer (Inis Óirr), nearest to County Clare (reached from Doolin), is the smallest of the Aran Islands at just over 3km (2 miles) across, and has a splendid 15th-century fort built by a chieftain of the O'Brien clan. **Inishmaan** (Inis Meáin), in

Left: Aran Island houses are built low to give maximum protection from bad weather

Right: Seaweed is gathered to be used as fertiliser on the rocky fields

- *Skerrett* by Liam O'Flaherty – titanic, tragic struggle between Inishmore's priest and schoolmaster, written by a native and based on a true story.
- *The Aran Islanders* by J M Synge – classic account of the islands and their people at the turn of the 20th century, garnered during the playwright's sojourns on Inishmaan, 1898–1902.

the middle, is 5km (3 miles) across and is the most traditional and the most remote.

Inishmore

For island specialists with a couple of days in hand, Inishmaan and Inisheer offer unforgettable delights. But most visitors will opt for **Inishmore** (Inis Mór), the biggest Aran Island at 13km (8 miles) long and the most easily accessible.

Inishmore has a small port at Kilronan, and a tiny airstrip. You could drive from Galway to Rossaveal for a 40-minute ferry crossing, or fly over from Connemara Airport, just outside Galway City, and be in Inishmore in six minutes. There is a heritage centre at Kilronan to introduce you to the Aran Islands.

The island's chief attraction is the clifftop fort of **Dunaengus** with its three giant rings of battlements; but the island is covered in pre-Christian and early Christian remains. Take time to walk, talk, listen, sit and stare. Even in Ireland you won't find a more peaceful spot.

TAKING A BREAK

Stop for lunch in **Joe Watty's** friendly pub in Inishmore's tiny port of Kilronan.

➕ 198 C5

Tourist Information Offices
✉ Kilronan, Inishmore ☎ 099 61263; www.visitaranislands.com ⏰ All year
✉ Aras Fáilte, Forster Street, Galway
☎ 091 537700; www.discoverireland.ie/west ⏰ All year

Dunaengus
☎ 099 61088 ⏰ Mar–Oct daily 10–6; Nov–Feb 10–4 🎟 Free

THE ARAN ISLANDS (OILEÁIN ÁRANN): INSIDE INFO

Top tips Tours include Dunaengus and Seven Churches. A bus leaves for Dunaengus Mon–Sat at 10, 1 and 4 in summer (last bus 2:30 in winter).
- If you are planning to visit Inishmaan, **check the weather forecast first**. Fog, mist or high winds can suspend all travel between island and mainland.
- Note that there is only one ATM on Inis Mór, in the Spar Supermarket.

Hidden gem On Inishmore, about 6km (4 miles) east of Dunaengus, is the less visited stronghold of **Dún Dúchathair**, spectacularly set on the cliff edge.

❸ Connemara

Connemara, in northwest County Galway, is the romantic heart of the west, a harsh land of boggy fields, knobbly mountains and savage sea coasts. Dublin schoolkids come here to learn Irish; the rest of us visit for the wild and beautiful scenery. But make no mistake, this is a tough place to live, with poor soil stretched thinly over beds of unyielding granite. As the locals say: "You can't eat scenery."

North of Galway stretches the immense inland sea of **Lough Corrib**. Here angling-oriented Oughterard is a pretty spot to base yourself for good trout fishing, while **Cong Abbey** on the north shore is a glorious little 12th-century building.

West of here is Joyce Country, so named because much of the population were of the Joyce clan, where the sister ranges of the **Maumturk Mountains** and the magnificent **Twelve Bens** (or Twelve Pins) pierce the sky with quartzite peaks. This is wonderful walking country, bounded on the north by mountains sweeping down to Killary Harbour.

The Far West

Going west again, you are confronted by classic Connemara landscapes, a hard land of wide bog vistas, rugged brown hills and innumerable little lakes. **Clifden**, a Victorian holiday resort, sits out west in the centre of a wheel of craggy coastline, where a coast road crawls around the indentations. Follow it east, stopping at **Roundstone** to visit the workshop

The Twelve Bens rise above the Connemara National Park

A lonely cottage within the Connemara National Park

at Roundstone Musical Instruments, where Malachy Kearns makes the world's best *bodhráns* (goatskin drums). Then carry on in increasingly desolate scenery towards Galway City. Before getting there, spare a couple of hours to turn right at Costelloe (Casla), where a causeway road takes you through the Irish-speaking islands of **Lettermore** (Leitir Moir), **Gorumna** (Garumna) and **Lettermullan** (Leitir Mealláin).

TAKING A BREAK

The Steam Coffee House in Clifden is a lively, inexpensive place to eat. In Roundstone, **Brown's** restaurant in the Alcock & Brown Hotel serves excellent, freshly prepared cuisine.

194 B1

Tourist Information Office
Áras Fáilte, Forster Street, Galway City ☎ 091 537700; www.discoverireland.ie/west

CONNEMARA: INSIDE INFO

Top tips To get straight from Galway City to Clifden, the "capital" of West Connemara, take N59. This road whisks you straight there on an 80km (50-mile) run through the heart of the region.
■ Bring your fly and coarse rods if you are an angler; the **coastal rivers of Connemara are some of the best in Ireland** for salmon, and the loughs provide excellent trout fishing.
■ If you are visiting in August, try to get to the **Clifden Show**, where appealing, long-haired Connemara ponies are brought for sale.

Hidden gem The sixth-century oratory on **St Macdara's Island** (Oileán Mhic Dara), 9.5km (6 miles) south of Roundstone (where you charter boats to the island).

One to miss Avoid **Salt Hill in holiday season**, when it becomes a crowded, very average seaside resort. There are better, quieter beaches a little further west.

4 West Mayo

West Mayo is one of Ireland's most atmospheric corners. While not exactly undiscovered, it is far enough distant from Dublin and walled in by serious enough mountains and boglands to retain (and flaunt) its own character.

Clew Bay and Westport

Centrepiece of the region is broad **Clew Bay**, reputed to have 365 islands. Certainly there are several dozen of them, little drumlins (heaps of Ice Age rubble) with grassy backs turned to the land and yellow clay teeth bared to the west. At the mouth of Clew Bay is **Clare Island**, humpbacked and greenly beautiful, a great place to spend a few days away from it all; a boat service from Roonagh Quay on the southwestern extremity of the bay takes, depending on the weather, between 30 minutes to an hour to reach the island.

On Clew Bay's south shore stands the 765m (2,510-foot) cone-shaped mountain of **Croagh Patrick** (known locally as "The Reek"), Ireland's Holy Mountain, focus of a massed annual pilgrimage and one of Ireland's classic hill hikes (➤ 176–177). The top of The Reek is the best vantage point to view Clew Bay.

At the southeastern corner of Clew Bay lies **Westport**, a small town of great charm and character, planned in the latter part of the 18th century by celebrated Georgian architect James Wyatt at the request of the Marquess of Sligo, on whose estate it was built. **Westport House** (1730–34),

White-washed cottages sit on a slope on Achill Island

beautifully furnished and with a fine collection of paintings, is worth a look around, and its grounds are lovely. A zoo and atmospheric dungeons are a bonus for visitors with children. But the great attraction of Westport is its town life – gossip, storytelling, music-making. It is one of the best towns in Ireland for traditional music and each year, in late September/early October, hosts an excellent arts festival, showcasing home-grown and invited talent.

Out at the northwest corner of Clew Bay is **Achill Island**, a big ragged outline attached to the mainland by a road bridge across Achill Sound (Gob an Choire). This Irish-speaking island, superbly mountainous, is Ireland's largest. You can climb 672m (2,205-foot) Slieve More, Achill's highest peak, from Doogort (Dumha Goirt) on the north coast, or join a boat rental party for a jaw-dropping inspection

Trawmore Beach on Achill Island, looking towards the dramatic Minaun Cliffs

of some of Ireland's highest cliffs at the island's northwestern tip. Boats can be rented from Doogort Pier; for information contact Alice's Harbour Inn tourist office (tel: 098 45384).

Country Life Museum

Over near Castlebar is the only national museum outside Dublin, the **National Museum of Ireland – Country Life**, appropriately located in one of Ireland's most rural counties. It contains the national Folklore Collection, comprising around 50,000 objects, and the displays reflect traditional rural life in Ireland between 1850 and 1950. The specially built museum is in the grounds of Turlough Park House, which is itself open to the public to show how the landowners lived

TAKING A BREAK

Stop for a drink at **Molloy's** pub in Westport, in the High Street. Matt Molloy, flute-player with the celebrated Chieftains band, often sits in with the musicians when he's at home. Alternatively, try **Quay Cottage** on the harbour (➤ 140).

➕ 194 C2

Tourist Information Office
✉ James Street, Westport, Co Mayo ☎ 098 25711;
www.discoverireland.ie/west

Westport House
➕ 194 C2 ☎ 098 27780/27766; www.westporthouse.ie 🕐 House and gardens: Apr–Sep daily 11:30–5:30; Mar Sat Sun 11:30–5:30. Attractions: Jun–Aug daily 11:30–5; also Easter holidays, May bank holiday and Sundays 11:30–5 💷 Expensive

National Museum of Ireland – Country Life
➕ 195 D2 ✉ Turlough Park, Castlebar, Co Mayo ☎ 094 903 1773;
www.museum.ie 🕐 Tue–Sat 10–5, Sun 2–5 💷 Free

At Your Leisure

5 Bunratty Castle and Folk Park

Conveniently near to Shannon Airport (west of Limerick City), this complex is aimed squarely at a tourist market. There are nightly mead'n'minstrels medieval banquets in the castle (reservations are essential) – great fun if you're in a jolly mood, and a crowded "19th-century Irish village" in the grounds with costumed guides and demonstrations of traditional skills. Come here well out of season, however, and you can appreciate the atmosphere and the authentic touches without having your toes trodden on. The castle itself, built in about 1425, is a very fine restoration, with plenty of good tapestries and beautiful furniture, some dating back as far as the building.

➕ 199 D4 ✉ Bunratty, Co Clare ☎ 061 711200; www.shannonheritage.com ⏰ Bunratty Castle: daily 9–4. Folk Park: Jan–May, Sep–Dec daily 9–5:30 (last admission 4:15); Jun–Aug Mon–Fri 9–5:30, Sat–Sun 9–6 (last admission 5:15) 💶 Expensive

Bunratty Castle was restored during the 1950s

6 Craggaunowen

At Craggaunowen, by a lake 21km (13 miles) north of Bunratty, the story of the Celts in Ireland is told by costumed guides amid clever reconstructions of Celtic buildings that include a *crannóg* or lake dwelling, a stone ring fort, round thatched huts and burial places. The leather-hulled boat *Brendan*, built by adventurer Tim Severin and sailed by him from the Dingle Peninsula to Newfoundland in 1976–77, is on display: it was this voyage that showed how St Brendan might have discovered America back in the sixth century AD.

➕ 199 D4 ✉ Quin, Co Clare ☎ 061 711200; www.shannonheritage.com ⏰ May–Sep daily 10–5 (last admission 4) 💶 Moderate

7 Clonmacnoise

Clonmacnoise is one of Ireland's finest and most interesting ecclesiastical sites. Founded by St Ciaran, it was the most influential centre in pre-Norman Europe in its day. Several Irish kings are buried here. Within the site are two Round Towers (the lightning-blasted 10th-

century O'Rourke's Tower and the almost perfect MacCarthy Tower of 1124), seven ancient churches and a largely 14th-century cathedral. Of three notable high crosses, the best is the richly carved Cross of the Scriptures, also known as the Great Cross, which dates from the early 10th century and stands over 4m (13 feet) tall.

🔢 199 F5 ⊠ On R444, north of Shannonbridge, Co Offaly ☎ 090 967 4195; www.heritageireland.ie ⊙ Mid-May to mid-Sep 9–7; mid-Mar to mid-May and mid-Sep to Oct 10–6; Nov to mid-Mar 10-5:30 ⊌ Moderate

🎱 Thoor Ballylee

I the poet William Yeats,
With old millboards and sea-green
slates
And smithy work from the Gort forge
Restored this tower for my wife
George.
And may these characters remain
When all is ruin once again.

This inscription at Thoor Ballylee tells the story of the medieval stone tower house bought by W B Yeats in 1916 for £35, and intermittently inhabited (and written about) by him. It is now a beautifully restored museum housing Yeats memorabilia and first editions. An audioguide (available in several languages) brings the history alive and you can also take a riverside walk to an ancient mill.

🔢 199 D5 ⊠ Gort, Co Galway ☎ 091 631436 (winter 091 537700) ⊙ Jun–Sep Mon–Sat 9:30–5 ⊌ Moderate

🎱 Galway City

Galway is one of the fastest growing cities in Europe and it is a thriving place with a lively atmosphere thanks to its university and the large number of job-providing industries that have sprung up around the town. During Galway Arts Festival late in July, and the Races that follow it, is a good time to visit. Everything centres on Eyre Square, which was recently given a multi-million euro makeover. In the streets to the south and west you'll find most of the bars, and some good restaurants and

The door of one of the eight ruined churches at Clonmacnoise

shops. Galway City Museum, which opened in 2006 behind the city's famous Spanish Arch, gives a good insight into Galway's past through a collection of historical artefacts and works of art.

🔢 199 D5

Galway City Museum
⊠ Galway City Museum, Spanish Parade, Galway City ☎ 091 532460; www.galwaycitymuseum.ie ⊙ Daily 10–5 ⊌ Free

🔟 Strokestown Park House, Garden & Famine Museum

Allow a good half-day to explore this fascinating place. The big, white-fronted Palladian mansion, approached through a grand arch, dates back to the 1660s, though it

---

FOR KIDS

Leisureland, a modern pool complex in Salt Hill, has a waterslide, Treasure Cove complete with pirate ship, a tropical beach pool, playground and amusement park.
⊠ Salt Hill, Galway ☎ 091 521455 ⊙ Opening times vary. To avoid disappointment phone first ⊌ Moderate

was remodelled in the 1730s. The original 18th-century furnishings are still in place. Tunnels concealed the movement of servants from the patrician gaze of the Mahon family, owners of Strokestown. There was even a gallery constructed around the kitchen so that the lady of the house could observe what went on without being seen herself.

Money and privilege did not save Major Denis Mahon. He was murdered on his estate during the Great Famine of 1845–50 after he had tried to evict most of his starving tenants and ship them off to America. An excellent, if harrowing, Famine Museum, in the old stable yard, tells of the tragic events. Outside in the grounds is a fine garden with a stunning herbaceous border.

➕ 195 F2 ✉ Strokestown, Co Roscommon
☎ 071 963 3013; www.strokestownpark.ie
🕑 Mid-Mar to Oct daily 10:30–5:30; Nov to mid-Mar by appointment 💷 Expensive

⑪ Nephin Beg Mountains

These roadless mountains in north-west Mayo fill a triangle of 200sq km (78sq miles) north of Westport,

Strokesdown Park House is home to the Famine Museum

flanked by the wild Atlantic coast on the west and the great bog of Bellacorick on the east. It is the remotest range in Ireland, crossed by one dramatic and demanding footpath, the 48km (30-mile) Bangor Trail from Newport to Bangor Erris. The path can be followed at any time of year, but only by experienced walkers with plenty of stamina. Don't attempt it on your own or in bad weather. For more information, contact the tourist office in Westport, tel: 098 25711.

➕ 194 C2

⑫ Céide Fields

A pyramidal visitor centre, housing a surprisingly good exhibition, is the focal point of the world's largest Stone Age site – 1,500 hectares (3,705 acres) of stone-walled fields, enclosures, dwelling areas and megalithic tombs dating back approximately 5,000 years. All have been painstakingly unearthed by archaeologists since the 1970s from the blanket bog that swallowed them.

➕ 194 C3 ✉ Ballycastle, Co Mayo
☎ 096 43325; www.heritageireland.ie
🕑 Jun–Sep daily 10–6; mid-Mar to May and Oct–Nov 10–5 💷 Inexpensive

FOUR LONELY HEADLANDS WITH WONDERFUL VIEWS
- Malin Head, Donegal ➕ 196 C1
- Achill Head, Achill Island, Mayo ➕ 194 B2
- Mace Head, Connemara, Galway ➕ 194 B1
- Hags Head, Clare ➕ 198 C4

ALCOCK AND BROWN

Just off R341 coast road south of Clifden in western Connemara, a cairn stands in Derrigimlagh bog as a monument to Sir John Alcock and Sir Arthur Whitten Brown. It was here that their Vickers-Vimy biplane came to rest on its nose on 15 June, 1919, having completed the first non-stop flight across the Atlantic.

🔟 Sligo

Sligo is a delightful town, full of history and well supplied with restaurants and pubs. The small library, museum and art gallery, located inside a former Presbyterian, Gothic Revival church, contain paintings by Jack Yeats and manuscripts of poems by his brother, William Butler; the brothers spent many of their holidays with cousins in Sligo, a place they loved (► 178–180 for a tour of Yeats Country). An annual Yeats Summer School fills the town with fans of the poet each August. There's superb medieval stonework to see in Sligo's only surviving medieval building, the ruined **Dominican Friary** church of **Sligo Abbey**.

Among the town's other attractions are Hargadon's – a classic pub where chat is firmly on the agenda – and **Sheela-na-gig**, where there are excellent sessions of traditional music; and opposite the Court House in Teeling Street the much-photographed name plate of the aptly named solicitors, Argue and Phibbs, who once had their offices here.

➕ 195 E3

Read the runes on Sligo's monument to W B Yeats

Tourist Information Centre
✉ Aras Reddan, Temple Street ☎ 071 916 1201; www.discoverireland.ie/northwest

🔢 Southern Donegal

Donegal forms the northwestern corner of Ireland almost cut off from the Republic to which it belongs by the thrusting heel of Fermanagh in Northern Ireland. Of all the counties of western Ireland, it is probably the least explored, but if you enjoy rugged and lonely country and have time to spare, it shouldn't be missed.

Donegal's southwest coast is particularly spectacular. Along here, lying some 120km (75 miles) west of Donegal town, you will find the village of **Killybegs**. This is a big fishing port where fish-processing factories line the roads and sturdy red and-blue trawlers ride side by side in the harbour. Beyond lies a wild landscape of heathery hillsides, craggy headlands, pine forests and side roads that lead along coastal inlets. In Carrick (An Charraiag) a left turn (signed "Teelin Pier") takes

OFF THE BEATEN TRACK

Out beyond Clifden in westernmost Connemara lies the village of Claddaghduff. You can cross the sands here at low tide, with the aid of markers, to Omey Island, a secluded place where you'll find a hidden church, a holy well, ancient burial grounds and a beautiful circular walk. Keep an eye on the time – and tide – for getting back. For tide information contact the Connemara Walking Centre in Clifden, tel: 095 21379.

you via "Bunglass: The Cliffs" signs to a steep gated lane. This climbs to a thrilling viewpoint high above the cliffs of Slieve League (Sliabh Liag), rearing some 600m (1,970 feet) out of the sea in a blotched wall of yellow, black, orange and brown.

Now the main road swoops across wild bogland to **Glencolumbkille** (Gleann Cholm Cille), a Gaeltacht village, huddled in a long green valley under rugged headlands. St Columba, one of Ireland's patron saints who later went to Iona, established a monastery here, and the secluded valley is full of monuments that attest to its Christian heritage: stone slabs and pillars incised with crosses, cairns, early Christian chapels. Annually on 9 June pilgrims walk a 15-part Stations of the Cross route that links up several of these monuments. Glencolumbkille is an exceptionally peaceful and haunting place. Return via Ardara, and the mountain road back to Donegal town.

➕ 195 E4

🔢 Glenveagh National Park

Walkers and nature lovers come to Donegal to hike and catch sight of golden eagles in Glenveagh National Park. The visitor centre is located inside Glenveagh Castle, a 19th-century castellated Scottish baronial-style mansion beside Lough Veagh.

Visitors can take tours of the interior or join organized walks in the park.

➕ 196 B5 ✉ Churchill, Letterkenny ☎ 074 913 7090; www.glenveaghnationalpark.ie
🕐 Visitor centre: Mar–Oct daily 10–6:30; Nov–Feb 9–5

🔢 Inishowen Peninsula

Inishowen's flattened spear-blade shape forms the northernmost tip of Ireland, and is even more isolated than Donegal's southwestern coast. Northeast of lively party town Letterkenny you pass **Grianan of Aileach** in the neck of the peninsula, a circular stone fort 6m (20 feet) high, perched high on a hill overlooking Lough Swilly. Grianan of Aileach was sacked in 1101 by Murtagh O'Brien, King of Munster, who ensured its demolition by ordering his soldiers to remove a stone for every sack of provisions they carried. From here the road runs north past the beach at Buncrana into the bog and hills of northern Inishowen. Up at the peak of the peninsula you climb to the old signal-tower on **Malin Head** where there is nothing between you and the Scottish islands of the Outer Hebrides 160km (100 miles) to the north.

➕ 196 C5

The Donegal coastline is one of the quieter corners of Ireland

Where to...
Eat and Drink

Prices

Expect to pay per person for a meal, excluding drinks and service

€ under €15   €€ €15–€30   €€€ over €30

THE BURREN

Aillwee Cave Café €

Everything is fresh and home-made at this friendly eatery in one of Ireland's premiere attractions. After visiting the 2 million-year-old cave have a tasty snack or lunch. Pick from a long list: soup, sandwiches, rolls, salads, cakes and biscuits. Or check out the potato bar, where Ireland's staple comes with a choice of scrumptious fillings. Ice cream, popcorn and more to takeout, too.

➕ 199 D5 ⊠ Ballyvaughan, Co Clare
☎ 065 707 7036; www.aillweecave.ie
🕙 Daily in peak season from 10am

Hylands Burren Hotel €–€€

This delightful old family-run establishment, close to Ballyvaughan harbour, has open fires, well-crafted furniture and a welcoming atmosphere. Its reputation for good food is growing – specialities include freshly caught seafood, Burren lamb, organic vegetables and herbs, and local farmhouse cheeses. Caring service and a genuine sense of hospitality add to the enjoyment.

➕ 199 D5 ⊠ Ballyvaughan, Co Clare
☎ 065 707 7037; www.hylandsburren.com
🕙 Bar food: daily 12:30–9; closed 2 Jan–2 Feb. Restaurant: 7–9; closed Christmas

Sheedy's Country House Hotel €€

The hotel has been run by the Sheedy family for generations, and their hands-on approach shows in the attractive furnishings and open fires. However, good food is perhaps the major draw, with dishes such as traditional chowders and crab salads in the Seafood Bar, and more formal dining in the Sheedy's Restaurant. Exacting standards of produce and cooking apply to both, including using fresh fish from the Burren Smokehouse nearby.

➕ 198 C5 ⊠ Lisdoonvarna, Co Clare ☎ 065 707 4026; www.sheedys.com 🕙 Restaurant/Seafood bar: daily 6:45pm–8:45pm; closed mid-Oct to Easter

GALWAY CITY AND SURROUNDING AREA

Kirby's of Cross Street €–€€

This dashingly informal restaurant/bar/café is next door to one of Galway's leading pubs. Busker Browne's and The Slate House. Lots of light wood, bare tables, and cheerful young staff give it a youthful atmosphere. The attractively presented contemporary cuisine is based on Irish themes, seasoned with influences from further afield.

➕ 199 D5 ⊠ Cross Street, Galway ☎ 091 569404; www.kirbysrestaurant.com 🕙 Daily 12:30–2:30, 5:30–10:30

Moran's Oyster Cottage €–€€€

An idyllic thatched pub on Galway Bay, with its own oyster beds, Moran's attracts a loyal following from all over Ireland and beyond. The seafood is wonderful, and the native oysters – in season from September to April – are a treat. You can have the farmed Gigas oysters all year, however, along with other specialities like seafood chowder, smoked salmon and delicious crab sandwiches and salads.

➕ 199 D5 ⊠ The Weir, Kilcolgan, Co Galway ☎ 091 796113; www.moransoystercottage.com 🕙 Bar food: 12–10

White Gables Restaurant €€€

Open stonework and soft lighting create a soothing atmosphere in this attractive restaurant on the main street of Moycullen, 8km (5 miles) north of Galway City. The hearty cooking is always good, with freshly made soups, specialities such as black and white pudding with wholegrain mustard sauce, and roast duckling with orange sauce. The traditional Sunday lunch is particularly popular with locals and visitors.

➕ **199 D5** ◻ **Moycullen, Co Galway** ☎ **091 555744; www.whitegables.com** ⏰ **Tue–Sat 7–10, Sun 12:30–2:30 (also open Mon mid-Jul to mid-Aug); closed 23 Dec–14 Feb**

ATHLONE

Wineport Lodge Restaurant €€€

Attractions are the 10 luxury guestrooms, the location on Lough Ree, the hospitality, and the seasonal menus. These are based on such local delicacies as Irish veal, game, fresh scallops, home-grown

herbs and wild mushrooms. The style of cooking is international and modern Irish, some creative vegetarian cooking and an Irish farmhouse cheeseboard. Bar food is available 1–5pm in summer.

➕ **195 F1** ◻ **Glasson, Nr Athlone, Co Westmeath** ☎ **090 439010; www.wineport.ie** ⏰ **Mon–Sat 6–10: Sun 3–5, 6–10**

CONNEMARA

O'Dowd's Seafood Bar and Restaurant €–€€

This traditional bar, overlooking the harbour in the pretty village of Roundstone, serves a good pint; the bar menu is reasonably priced. The restaurant offers more substantial meals, dominated by fish and seafood straight off the boat, including haddock, turbot, mussels and oysters. There is also a coffee shop serving Irish breakfast and speciality teas and coffee.

➕ **194 B1** ◻ **Roundstone, Co Galway** ☎ **095 35809; www.odowdsrestaurant.com**

⏰ **Bar food: noon–9.30. Restaurant: Apr–Sep 12–10; Oct–Mar 12–3, 6–9:30**

Steam Coffee House €

Steam Coffee House is a very welcome, child-friendly offshoot of the award-winning High Moors restaurant, which enjoys a fine reputation. This is the place to come for soup and a sandwich, puddings, ice-creams or just a cup of coffee.

➕ **194 B1** ◻ **Courtyard Shopping Centre, Clifden Station House, Clifden** ☎ **095 21526; www.clifdenstationhouse.com** ⏰ **Daily 10–6; late openings Thu and Fri 6–8**

WESTPORT

Quay Cottage €€

This stone waterside restaurant never fails to delight. Its maritime theme is strongly reinforced by the imaginative menu, with such items as chowder and seafood platter. There is much else of interest, including mountain lamb and creative vegetarian options. Tempting desserts or a farmhouse

cheese selection, and freshly brewed coffee make a fitting finale.

➕ **194 C2** ◻ **The Harbour, Westport, Co Mayo** ☎ **098 26412; www.quaycottage.com** ⏰ **Daily 6pm–late; closed 24–26 Dec and mid-Jan to mid-Feb**

CAVAN

MacNean House and Restaurant

€€€

Known all over Ireland for its superb food when it was a laid-back bistro owned by MacNean's parents, in 2007 Nevan transformed its still the current multi-award-winning establishment. Locally sourced ingredients and infinite care are still what underpins the quality at this winner of the Best Chef and Best Celebrity Chef at the Irish Restaurant Awards 2009.

➕ **196 B3** ◻ **Main Street, Blacklion, Co Cavan** ☎ **071 9853022; www.macneanrestaurant.com** ⏰ **Jun–Sep Wed–Sat 6:30–9.30, Sun 12:30–3:30, 7–8:30; Oct–May Wed–Sat 6:30pm–9.30pm, Sun 12:30–3:30; closed one week over Christmas and all Jan**

Where to... Stay

Where to... Stay

SLIGO

Cromleach Lodge €€€

Fine views from this modern building on a hill overlooking Lough Arrow are a bonus: Moira and Christy Tighe's hospitality ensures comfort and relaxation for guests, many drawn by Moira's superb food. The best of local ingredients – organic vegetables and herbs, goat's cheese, or succulent loin of local lamb – underlie a light, elegant style with excellent saucing. Simple table settings complement the growing number of mouthwatering house specialities.

➕ 196 A2 ☒ Castlebaldwin, Co Sligo ☎ 071 916 5155; www.cromleach.com ◉ Restaurant: Mon–Sat 12–6, 6–9, Sun 12–4, 7–8. Bar food: Mon–Thu 11:30–9, Fri–Sat 11:30–6

Fiddlers Creek €€

Good, wholesome food is served in the dining room and snug bar. Some tables have views over the river. As well as steak, chicken and fish dinner options there's a range of salads and sandwiches at lunchtime. Twists on classics give the menu an interesting slant – for example fresh Irish salmon marinated in Cajun spices.

➕ 196 A2 ☒ Rockwood Parade, Sligo, Co Sligo ☎ 071 914 1866; www.fiddlerscreek.ie ◉ Mon–Sat 12–3:30, 5–9:30, Sun 12:30–9:30

DONEGAL

The Red Door Restaurant €€

Reopened under new management in 2009, this cosy restaurant overlooking Lough Swilly has already re-earned its former popularity. Tuck into plates of Irish salmon, smoked haddock, fillet steak or duck, but save room for comforting desserts like crumble and rice pudding.

➕ 195 C5 ☒ Carrowmullin Fahan, Inishowen, Co Donegal ☎ 074 936 0289; www.thereddoor.ie ◉ Thu–Sat 6–11, Sun 1–4:30, 5:30–10:30

Prices

Expect to pay per night for a double room
€ under €70 €€ €70–€130 €€€ over €130

THE BURREN

Gregans Castle €€€

This remote hotel on the inland road between Ballyvaughan and Lisdoonvarna may seem as stark as the landscape, but appearances are deceptive. In fact, warmth, elegance and tranquillity are the keynotes, both in spacious public rooms and luxurious accommodation. Non-residents are welcome in the restaurant, and also for lunch or afternoon tea in the Corkscrew Room bar.

➕ 199 D5 ☒ Ballyvaughan, Co Clare ☎ 065 707 7005; www.gregans.ie

◉ Restaurant: daily 7–8:30pm, light meals from noon; closed Nov to mid-Feb

Temple Gate Hotel €€–€€€

This hotel, right in the centre of Ennis, is a clever conversion of a building that formerly served as a gentleman's residence, then a convent. It retains some of its Gothic-style features. The 73 rooms are classic in style but the facilities are modern with neat private bathrooms. There is a restaurant and a pub with music on weekends.

➕ 199 D4 ☒ The Square, Ennis, Co Clare ☎ 065 682 3300; www.templegatehotel.com

GALWAY CITY AND SURROUNDING AREA

Ardilaun House Hotel €€–€€€

Set in wooded grounds about five minutes' drive from the city centre, Ardilaun House Hotel has elegantly furnished, spacious public rooms, plus a leisure centre with an indoor pool and hydro spa. The bedrooms are well decorated – those with bay views are the most popular, though others are equally attractive. The pleasant dining room overlooks the pretty gardens.

✚ 199 D5 ☒ Taylor's Hill, Galway ☎ 091 521433; www.theardilaunhotel.ie

The g €€€

This modern hotel has been the talk of the town for its Philip Treacy interiors, which ooze conetmporary, funky glamour, bold colours bounciong off the large mirrors and chandeleier. Bedrooms are contrastingly calm and mostly neutral, and the spa lets you wind down further. Although

it is situated in the industrial outskirts of Galway, you come here to indulge yourself, not for the charming location.

✚ 199 D5 ☒ Wellpark, Galway ☎ 091 865200; www.theghotel.ie

Jurys Inn Galway €€

This good-value choice, perfectly set by the river and the bustling Spanish Arch area of Galway City centre, provides a high standard of basic accommodation. Rooms are large and provide every comfort and convenience: neat bathrooms, TV, phone and hospitality tray – but with no room service or other extras. However, there's a pleasant bar, a restaurant/coffee bar, and adjoining parking.

✚ 199 D5 ☒ Quay Street, Galway ☎ 091 566444; www.galwayhotels.jurysinns.com

Mallmore House €€

A really delightful country house bed-and-breakfast in lovely gardens, situated a couple of miles outside the Connemara "capital" of Clifden

in a beautiful wild part of County Galway. Friendly, approachable and very helpful hosts, turf fires to warm you, and breakfasts that fuel you for a day's exploring.

✚ 194 B1 ☒ Ballyconneely Road, Clifden, Co Galway ☎ 095 21460; www.mallmore.com

ATHLONE

Hodson Bay Hotel €€€

Overlooking Lough Ree, this hotel adjoins Athlone Golf Club and has lovely lake and island views. Amenities include boating, fishing and a leisure centre. Comfortable bedrooms are decorated in a bright contemporary style, and there are well-finished bathrooms, plus all the necessary extras (phone, TV, hospitality tray). The excellent L'Escale restaurant offers Irish dishes alongside more exotic options such as rattlesnake.

✚ 195 F1 ☒ Hodson Bay, Athlone, Co Westmeath ☎ 090 644 2000; www.hodsonbayhotel.com

WESTPORT

Breaffy House €€

A handsome Victorian house in nearly 40ha (100 acres) of landscaped gardens and wooded grounds on the outskirts of Castlebar. Breaffy House is not only a good comfortable hotel, but also a spa with mud- and steam-baths, swimming pools, sauna, dance studio and all manner of massages and other relaxing and renewing treatments. So if the Mayo weather turns a bit "soft", you can still have a great time here!

✚ 195 D2 ☒ Castlebar, Co Mayo ☎ 094 902 2033; www.breaffyhousecastlebar.com

Carrabaun House €

On the road out towards Galway, a couple of minutes' drive from the traditional music town of Westport, this bed-and-breakfast has great views of the Holy Mountain of Croagh Patrick. It is a first-class stopover, with friendly hosts who'll really try their best for you.

Particularly good are the breakfasts – try the fabulous Carrabaun porridge with a little drop of magic, or sample their salmon with soda bread, a pairing fit for an angel's cookbook.

🚩 194 C2 ⊠ Leenane Road, Westport, Co Mayo ☎ 098 26196; www.anu.ie/carrabaunhouse

SLIGO

Markree Castle €€

Home to the Cooper family for 350 years and set in park and farmland, this is a real traditional Irish castle. A huge welcoming log fire always burns brightly in the lofty hall – generosity with heating is one of the castle's most attractive features. There's a very beautiful dining room (non-residents welcome) for more formal dining and a large double drawing room where delicious light food, including afternoon tea, is served. The full Irish Breakfast is not to be missed, and be sure to try the freshly made

brown soda bread. Two floors of attractively furnished bedrooms provide guests with all the necessary comforts and amenities and there is the added bonus of pleasant parkland views.

🚩 195 E3 ⊠ Collooney, Co Sligo ☎ 071 916 7800; www.markreecastle.ie

DONEGAL

Kee's Hotel €€

Established as a coaching inn in 1845, and in the Kee family since 1892, this comfortable hotel is well placed for touring County Donegal. Rooms at the back of the hotel are quieter and more desirable than those at the front; some have views of the Blue Stack Mountains. There's an excellent leisure centre for guests and a stylish, fine restaurant, **The Looking Glass**, where imaginative Franco-Irish cuisine is served. There is often live music playing on Sunday nights.

🚩 196 B4 ⊠ Stranorlar, Ballybofey, Co Donegal ☎ 074 913 1018; www.keeshotel.ie

Where to...
Shop

A high proportion of the goods on sale in western Ireland are locally made. Ennis rewards a leisurely browse n uncrowded streets.

COUNTY CLARE

Custy's Music Shop in Ennis (Cookes Lane, tel: 065 682 1727) is the best place in the west to buy instruments and pick up news of local sessions. At Doolin, the **Doolin Crafts Gallery** (Ballyvoe, tel: 065 707 4309) sells a range of leatherware, ceramics, jewellery and clothing. Go 5km (3 miles) east to the spa town of Lisdoonvarna and you can visit the **Burren Smokehouse Ltd** (tel: 065 707 4432) to see how oak-smoking of Atlantic salmon is done (and buy a vacuum-packed side to take home).

GALWAY CITY

In Galway, a one-stop shop for the best in Irish design is **Judy Greene** (Kirwan's Lane, tel: 091 561753, www.judygreenepottery. com). If you're in the city on a Saturday, the **Galway Market** at St Nicholas Collegiate Church is a must: it sells everything from organic vegetables to preserves. The excellent **Kenny's Bookshop and Art Galleries** (High Street, tel: 091 709350, www.kennys.ie) is also worth a visit. It has five floors of Irish-interest books, mainly second-hand, as well as the Kerry Art Gallery. Also a bit different is **Claddagh Jewellers** (Eyre Square, tel: 091 562554), where you'll find a wide selection of traditional Celtic jewellery.

CONNEMARA

Connemara Marble Industries Ltd (Moycullen, tel: 091 555102) sells locally quarried marble items, and **Joyce's** of Recess (tel: 095 34734) has a range of quality goods. Musicians should head for **Roundstone Musical Instruments** (Roundstone, tel: 095 35808).

Clifden has good gift shops, including **The Celtic Shop and Tara Jewellers** established 1976 (tel: 095 21064) with gifts, clothing, and gold and silver Irish jewellery. At Avoca, Letterfrack, **Connemara Handcrafts** (tel: 095 41058), a branch of the Wicklow-based Avoca Handweavers, sells fabrics, clothing, crafts and specialist foods. Even better, perhaps, is **Kylemore Abbey**, where there's a good craft shop (tel: 095 41437) and an excellent informal restaurant.

Foxford Woollen Mills (Foxford, tel: 094 925 6756) is a good place to buy tweeds and blankets; there's a shop, a restaurant and a Visitor Centre, which re-creates the mill in former centuries.

Over at Achill Island you could take a break at **The Beehive** (Keel, tel: 098 43134), an attractive craft shop and restaurant that serves home-made food all day.

SLIGO AND DONEGAL

The counties of Sligo and Donegal are famous for sweaters, tweeds and parian china (so called after the marble from the Greek island of Paros, which it resembles), all widely available. Useful addresses include the **Donegal Craft Village** (tel: 074 972 2225), five minutes' walk from the town centre and **Magee's** (Donegal town, tel: 074 972 2660), renowned for tweeds; they also sell quality gifts and have a good self-service restaurant. Tiny, characterful **Ardara** is chock-full of shops selling keenly priced local knits and weaves.

Where to...
Be Entertained

MUSIC

You'll find great pubs in the west of Ireland doing organised and impromptu music sessions. In Ennis, try **Cruise's** (Abbey Street, tel: 065 684 1800) and **Preachers Pub** (Temple Gate Hotel, The Square, tel: 065 682 3300); **O'Connors** (tel: 065 707 4168) of Doolin is highly regarded, while **Vaughan's** of Kilfenora (tel: 065 708 8004) is famous for set dancing and music. Galway is packed with music pubs: **Tigh Neachtain** (Cross Street, tel: 091 568820) is one of the best. In early May, Kinvarra runs a **Cuckoo Fleadh**, with traditional music (www.cuckoofleadh.com). The **Galway Sessions** in June present traditional music at various pubs, including the **Crane Bar** (William Street West, tel: 091 587419) and **Taaffe's** (Shop Street, tel: 091 564066). Westport is noted for its music pubs (▶ 133). Sligo is another musical hot spot; **Furey's** offers traditional, country, jazz, blue grass and Latino (tel: 091 43825, www.fureys.ie). County Donegal hosts the **Ballyshannon International Folk Festival** (www.ballyshannonfolkfestival.com).

OUTDOOR ACTIVITIES

This region offers scenic drives, golf, cycling, horseback riding and horse racing. There's surfing on Atlantic beaches such as Strandhill on Sligo Bay (rent boards and suits from **Strandhill Surf School** (tel: 071 916 8483). Fishing is also superb, particularly in County Mayo.

Northern Ireland

Getting Your Bearings

As you explore the cliffs, hills, country lanes and city streets of Northern Ireland, you will find that all the attributes of landscape and people that make the Republic so appealing are here in abundance, along with a remarkably traffic-free road system and a good number of uncrowded visitor attractions.

Northern Ireland remains part of the United Kingdom, and no one coming here can be unaware of the deep divisions between loyalists, those who want to maintain links with Britain, and nationalists, who wish to sever them. As a guest north of the border, it's good to inform yourself about recent history. Violence and hatred flared during the past 30 years or so between small extremist sections of the nationalist and loyalist communities in Northern Ireland, and between hardline nationalists insisting on a united Ireland and the security forces of army and police whom they saw as reinforcing the North's links with Great Britain. This period of armed conflict in Ulster's history came to be known as "The Troubles". However, the 1998 Good Friday Agreement, signed by all the interested political parties, brought hope and peace, along with the establishment of a devolved Government of Northern Ireland made up of Ulster politicians from both sides of the divide. Optimism has returned to Northern Ireland, and with it a very welcome positive atmosphere of regeneration, and a renewed interest among visitors in all that this great place has to offer.

Belfast has its cheerful black humour, vibrant nightlife and superb Botanical Gardens. The east coast is carved by the Glens of Antrim into beautiful deep valleys, and the Antrim Coast in the north is celebrated for the Giant's Causeway, one volcanic extravaganza among many along this spectacular line of cliffs. Swing across the hair-raising Carrick-a-Rede rope bridge; take a hike over the wild Sperrin or Mourne mountains, watch the geese and wading birds on Strangford Lough, or lazily cruise the great inland waterway of Lough Erne among islands crammed with ancient churches, round towers and enigmatic stone carvings. And spare a day to enjoy welcoming and optimistic Derry.

Page 145: The Giant's Causeway in the evening sun

Londonderry Derry **7**

B48
B49

Lifford
BS36

Plumbridge

Newtownstewart A5

Ulster American Folk Park **8**

Drumquin

Omagh

A32 Dromore

A47

4 **Belleek Pottery**

4 **Lough Erne**

Irvinestown

Castle Coole

A4

BS2

Enniskillen Lisbellaw

Blacklion Belcoo

A32

9

Marble Arch Caves

10

Lisnaskea

A509 Upper Lough Erne

Florence Court

Swanlinbar

Newtownbutler

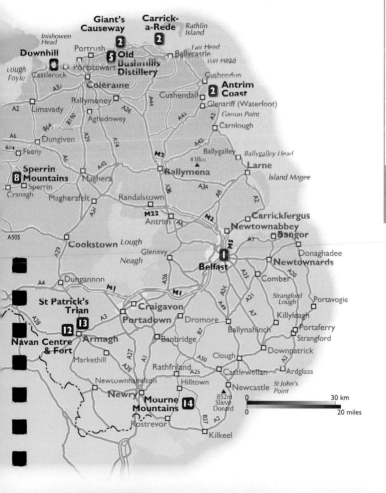

In Three Days

If you're not quite sure where to begin your travels, this itinerary recommends a practical and enjoyable short trip in Northern Ireland, taking in some of the best places to see using the Getting Your Bearings map on the previous page. For more information see the main entries.

Day 1

Morning
Explore **❶Belfast** (➤ 150–153), making sure not to miss the Grand Opera House (right), Botanic Gardens, Ulster Museum and political and cultural murals along the Shankill and Falls roads.

Afternoon
After an early lunch in the Victorian splendour of the Crown Liquor Saloon (➤ 167), head north around the spectacular Antrim Coast by way of the deep-cut **❷Glens of Antrim** (➤ 154). Stick to the minor coast road round Torr Head. Signposted turnings lead to **Carrick-a-Rede rope bridge** (below, ➤ 155), a nerve-tingling crossing above a sheer drop, and the **Giant's Causeway** (➤ 156), from whose slippery basalt promontory there are memorable cliff views. Overnight on the coast at Portstewart or Portrush.

Day 2

Morning
7 Derry City (➤ 164, 181) lies to the west – if you have a little more time, walk around the city walls. To continue the itinerary from Portstewart, head south via Coleraine and Limavady to Dungiven, then on to Feeny (B74). A further 5km (3 miles) south (B44), take the mountain road that crosses the rugged **8 Sperrin Mountains** (➤ 164) to reach Sperrin village. Head west along the Glenelly Valley for a drink and a snack at Leo McCullagh's pub in Plumbridge, then southeast to Newtonstewart and south to Omagh.

Afternoon
About 5km (3 miles) north of Omagh lies the **3 Ulster American Folk Park** (➤ 158–159), well worth an hour's exploration to see the carefully reconstructed houses and the striking emigration exhibition. From Omagh drive southwest (A32) to Irvinestown, then west on A35 or A47 to **4 Belleek** (➤ 160) and its world-famous pottery. A drive along the south shore of beautiful **Lough Erne** will land you in Enniskillen for the night.

Day 3

Morning
Drive east for 65km (40 miles) to Armagh City, where there is the excellent St Patrick's Trian and nearby historic **12 Navan** hill fort (➤ 165), then on to Newry and the A2 coast road. At Kilkeel bear left (B27) on side roads through the **14 Mountains of Mourne** (above, ➤ 166), then head northeast to Newcastle and Downpatrick with its cathedral and St Patrick's Grave.

Afternoon
Take the car ferry from Strangford to Portaferry, and drive north up the Ards Peninsula beside island-dotted and bird-haunted **Strangford Lough** (➤ 184–186); then continue from Newtownards into Belfast.

❶ Belfast

Belfast has had more than its share of bad publicity since the early 1970s. There's no denying that Northern Ireland's chief city has been the setting for some atrocious events, but visitors today need have no qualms about whether they will be welcome here. Belfast humour is black and mordant, but its people are particularly keen to put the bleak past behind them. Every new visitor is a symbol of a return to normal life, and especially welcome because of that. What you will find in Belfast is a fairly old-fashioned looking place, a city of the Industrial Revolution, with red-brick terraces and grandiose public buildings. It doesn't have the instant appeal of Dublin, but well repays a couple of days' exploration.

The City Centre and Golden Mile

Many of the attractions of Belfast city centre are within a few minutes' walk of each other. You could start and finish your sightseeing on Great Victoria Street at the **Crown Liquor Saloon** (➤ 167), now in the care of the National Trust, a splendidly maintained Victorian pub, complete with stained-glass windows, carved-wood booths, an elaborately tiled front, and a fine mosaic of a crown at the front door. The story goes that Patrick Flanagan, the pub's original owner and a passionate Irish nationalist, put the crown in that position so that anyone who wished could wipe their feet on it.

Belfast's ponderously magnificent 19th-century City Hall

Drinking in opulent surroundings at the Crown Liquor Saloon

Across from the Crown is the **Grand Opera House** of 1894, bombed and neglected in the past, but now restored to display its original grandeur, including gilt plaster and woodwork, a ceiling writhing with golden apes, and viewing boxes supported by gilt elephants with immense trunks. An extension was unveiled in 2006, controversially modern but which has increased and enhanced the entertainment space.

Great Victoria Street forms the west side of a triangle of streets known as the Golden Mile, where chic eateries and nightspots are clustered. At the top of the triangle is Donegall Square, with the remarkable **Linen Hall Library** – a historically important library for its age and associations with the rebellion by the United Irishmen in 1798. Visit to take in the thousands of well-thumbed books, atmosphere of studious hush, the Members' Room and Tea Room. Over Donegall Square revolves the magnificent **Wheel of Belfast**, a great spoked "bike wheel" with capsules suspended from its rim, from which there are mind-blowing views over the city. Nearby stands the recently restored grand Victorian **City Hall** of 1906 under a magnificent dome. Near here you'll find a fine memorial to the city's crewmen who lost their lives when the Belfast-built *Titanic* sank on 15 April, 1912. The interior of the City Hall is baroque, with a handsome central dome seen above a hollow galleried ceiling, and a Council Chamber full of carved wood, stained glass and padded red leather benches. The whole area has recently benefited from a huge makeover, with the smart new retail space, the **Victoria Square** – just what Belfast needs.

The University Area and Botanic

South of the city centre stands the early Victorian, mock-Tudor pile of **Queen's University**. Just beyond are Belfast's very enjoyable **Botanic Gardens**, a quiet and leafy spot with hundreds of tree species and the splendid Palm House, whose rounded prow and long side wings in cast iron and glass hold tropical vegetation in a hot, steamy atmosphere. Nearby is the 9m (30-foot)

EMERALD POET

Poet William Drennan (1754–1820) was born in Belfast. His output is forgotten these days but for one phrase, which has become the most fondly quoted cliché about Ireland – "The Emerald Isle".

Loyalist colours in the lower Newtownards Road

deep Tropical Ravine, housed inside a glass-roofed building dating from the 1880s, where fish and terrapins swim in the dripping shadows of cinnamon, dombeya, loquat and banana trees. In the extended and recently reopened **Ulster Museum**, alongside, the industrial history of Belfast is illustrated with mighty calendering (pressing) and fulling machines from the textile trade, photos of great ships being launched, tobacco and snuff samples – all reminders of the heavy industry that made this place.

Away from the Centre

Don't leave Belfast without seeing some of the **political murals** thrown up by the Troubles. Out west along the loyalist **Shankill Road** and nationalist **Falls Road** the polemic is fierce: even more so just east of the river in the Short Strand or Lower Newtownards roads. You can buy postcards showing the best examples of this "people's art".

On the eastern outskirts of Belfast is the imposing mansion of **Stormont**, home of the devolved Government of Northern Ireland. And north of the city centre in the shipyards stand **Samson and Goliath**, two giant yellow cranes that symbolize

---

BELFAST: INSIDE INFO

Top tip One of the best and quickest quickest ways to see Belfast is on a hop-on, hop-off, open-topped sightseeing bus tour. They leave regularly from Castle Street in the city centre.

Hidden gem Often seen, but seldom noticed with appreciation: the **Marks & Spencer department store** opposite the City Hall, a magnificent Italianate building in red Dumfries sandstone that used to house the Water Office.

One to miss Avoid the Golden Mile, and particularly Great Victoria Street, in the early hours at weekends if you are likely to get upset by the rowdy behaviour of young clubbers.

TROUBLES TAXIS

Regular buses were withdrawn in the 1970s due to hijackings, and though some services have been reinstated, black taxis still run what amount to cut-price minibus services to West Belfast. The drivers pack their vehicles, and the passengers split the fare.

the past industrial might and the dogged strength of this resilient city.

TAKING A BREAK

Stop for lunch at the **Crown Liquor Saloon** (➤ 167) and try the delicious "champ" – mashed potatoes and spring onions. **Made in Belfast** on Wellington Street is also a good place for light lunches.

🔁 197 E3
🛈 Belfast Welcome Centre, 47 Donegall Place ☎ 028 9024 6609; www.gotobelfast.com

Crown Liquor Saloon (NT)
✉ 46 Great Victoria Street ☎ 028 9027 9901; www.crownbar.com

Botanic Gardens
✉ Stranmillis Road/Botanic Avenue
☎ 028 9031 4762; www.belfastcity.gov.uk/parksandopenspaces
🕐 Gardens open 7:30am; check website for closing times Palm House and Tropical Ravine: Apr–Sep Mon–Fri 10–12, 1–5, Sat–Sun 1–5; Oct–Mar Mon–Fri 10–12, 1–4, Sat–Sun 1–3:45 🎟 Free

City Hall
✉ Donegall Square ☎ 028 9027 0456 🕐 Tours Mon–Fri 11, 2, 3, Sat 2, 3 🎟 Free

Linen Hall Library
🏛 17 Donegall Square North ☎ 028 9032 1707; www.linenhall.com
🕐 Library: Mon–Fri 9:30–5.30, Sat 9:30–4 🎟 Free

Ulster Museum
✉ Botanic Gardens ☎ 028 9038 3000; www.ulstermuseum.org.uk
🕐 Tue–Sun 10–5 🎟 Free

Wheel of Belfast
✉ Donegall Square East
☎ 028 9031 0607;
www.worldtouristattractions.co.uk
🕐 Sun–Thu 10–9, Fri 10–10, Sat 9am–10pm 🎟 Moderate

The splendid Palm House in the Botanic Gardens

FRAGRANT FLATS

Laganside, once a riverside slum area polluted by the smell from the mudflats at low tide, has been redeveloped as high-class residences. Lagan Weir keeps river levels constant and the stink away.

② The Antrim Coast

The Antrim Coast is Northern Ireland's best-known scenic attraction, with the Giant's Causeway as the plum in the pudding. But don't rush straight to these incredible volcanic rock formations; take your time getting there, and enjoy the beautiful journey north from Belfast through wild glens and along a wonderful coast road.

The Glens of Antrim

Take A2 north from Larne to Carnlough, a pretty little fishing harbour where the cliffs rise in a foretaste of what's in store. The road hugs the shore under steep hillsides for the next 16km (10 miles), curving into Red Bay at Waterfoot with some really striking big hills rearing inland. This is the place to turn aside up **Glenariff**, most spectacular of the series of deep glens carved into the basalt of North Antrim by rivers. Glenariff is bounded by granite cliffs over which waterfalls pour in rainy weather, a dark and rugged cleft. Drive up it and park at the Glenariff Forest Park Visitor Centre, amid mountain scenery. Various waymarked walking trails start from here: short garden and nature trails, a longer scenic trail, and a gorgeous 5km (3-mile) waterfall trail that leads you beside and over some of Glenariff's torrents.

The most spectacular of the Glens of Antrim, Glenariff has dozens of lovely waterfalls

Back on the coast road you go through neat little Cushendall. If you take A2 inland here, you can turn off left shortly and make a back-road loop up **Glenaan** by way of **Ossian's Grave** (► 157), before returning to the coast down quiet and lovely **Glendun**. From Cushendun among its trees there's an exhilarating alternative to A2 – a very rough and bouncy side road in marvellous coastal scenery via Torr Head to Ballycastle.

Carrick-a-Rede Rope Bridge

Carrick-a-Rede rope bridge is well signposted from Ballycastle. This clever cat's cradle of rope with a board floor used only to be open during the salmon fishing season, but since 2009 has been open all year, weather permitting. It's a good 800m (880-yard) walk from where you park to the bridge, with 161 stone steps, before you arrive at the entrance gate and look down on the nervous visitors swinging across the rope bridge, 25m (82 feet) above the sea. The National Trust has now "improved" the bridge's safety by installing a cage structure.

It's quite safe ...but you'll need some nerve to cross the Carrick-a-Rede rope bridge

The bridge is the only means of crossing the 20m (66-foot) gap between the cliff and the Carrick-a-Rede basalt stack offshore. The name means "rock-in-the-road" – the stack stands in the path of the salmon, who turn aside to pass it and swim into a net stretched out from the stack and anchored in the sea. It's a thrill to cross the bridge (come early or late to avoid the hordes), and a great photo opportunity.

The Giant's Causeway

So to the Giant's Causeway (the only World Heritage Site in Northern Ireland), a short distance along the coast. Here the cliffs are at their most spectacular as they rise almost 100m (330 feet) around a series of rocky bays. The Causeway itself is formed of some 37,000 basalt columns, mostly hexagonal, that slope in a narrowing and declining shelf into the sea. They were made by cooling lava after a volcanic eruption some 60 million years ago. Up in the cliffs of the bay are more formations. The most striking, reached by a footpath, is the Giant's Organ, a cluster of basalt "organ pipes" weathered into vertebra-like rings that rise 12m (40 feet) high. As for the Giant: he was the mythological giant Fionn mac Cumhaill (Finn McCool), who, legend has it, laid down the causeway as stepping stones to the island of Staffa.

Dare one say it? The Giant's Causeway, after all the publicity and raised expectations, can strike visitors as rather an anticlimax. Don't expect too much, and do make the footpath circuit if you can, up by the Organ and back along the clifftop footpath, to enjoy one of the best views of the Causeway.

Above: Cooled basalt formed the hexagonal columns of the Giant's Causeway

Right: High cliffs overlook the promontory of stumpy columns that noses out into the sea

TAKING A BREAK

The **Causeway Hotel Restaurant & Bar** is located as close as you can get to the Giant's Causeway. It offers classic pub grub and a cosy escape when the wind is lashing the shore outside.

Tourist Information Centre
197 E5 ✉ Sheskburn House, 7 Mary Street, Ballycastle ☎ 028 2076 2024; www.discovernorthernireland.com

Carrick-a-Rede Rope Bridge and Larrybane Visitor Centre
197 E5 ✉ On B15 between Ballycastle and Ballintoy ☎ 028 2076 9839; www.nationaltrust.org.uk ⏰ End Feb–end May, Sep–Oct 10–6; end may–Aug 10–7; Nov–end Feb 10:30–3:30 💷 Inexpensive

Giant's Causeway
197 D5 ✉ Giant's Causeway Centre, 3.2km (2 miles) north of Bushmills ☎ Visitor Centre: 028 2073 1582; shop: 028 2073 2972; www.nationaltrust.org.uk ⏰ Giant's Causeway always open for exploration 💷 Donations welcome

SPANISH TREASURE

The Spanish Armada galleon *Girona* was wrecked in Port na Spaniagh ("Spaniard's Bay"), just east of the Giant's Causeway in 1588. Out of 1,300 men, only five were saved. The treasure went to the bottom with the ship, and stayed there until 1968 when much of it was recovered: gold, silver, jewels, implements. The best of what was salvaged is on display in Belfast's Ulster Museum.

THE ANTRIM COAST: INSIDE INFO

Top tips If you want to avoid the 10-minute walk down the road from the Giant's Causeway Visitor Centre to the Causeway itself, **hop on the minibus**.
■ Don't take a large shoulder-bag or hold anything in your hands when you cross Carrick-a-Rede rope bridge, as you'll find you need both hands free for the crossing.

Hidden gem Signposted off A2 near the bottom of Glenaan is **Ossian's Grave**. This impressive "horned" cairn (with an entrance courtyard and two inner chambers) lies in a field at the top of a steep, rough lane better walked than driven, and commands a great view. Ossian was a warrior-poet, the son of the great hero Fionn mac cumhaill (Finn McCool).

One to miss The **coast road north** between Belfast and Larne is none too exciting; a better route is M2 to Junction 4, then the pleasant hill-and-valley A8 via Ballynure to Larne.

❸ Ulster American Folk Park

This collection of reconstructed and replica buildings gives a graphic idea of life in 18th- and 19th-century Ireland, of the miseries of emigration, and of the long, hard struggle that emigrants had to face before they could prosper in America.

The displays are divided into Ulster buildings, streets and dockside, and then American streets and buildings – roughly the Old World and New World.

Ulster Life

In the **Ulster section** you stroll among buildings brought from their original locations and rebuilt here. Among these are a **weaver's cottage** with a fixed loom, and a **Mass House** where Roman Catholics in the days of the Penal Laws (a collection of laws passed in the 18th century strictly limiting the rights of Catholics in all spheres) were permitted to attend the proscribed Mass. Don't miss **Castletown National School** with its graffiti-scarred desks – though it's a good idea to delay your visit if a school party is swarming there. Also here are the modest **homesteads** of two Irish emigrants who made spectacularly good in America: that of Judge Thomas Mellon (who emigrated in 1818), whose son Andrew Mellon founded the Pittsburgh steel industry, and John Joseph Hughes, Archbishop of New York and founder of St Patrick's Cathedral there. When the Folk Park's Visitor Centre was opened in 1980, the ceremony was attended by the benefactor, Dr Matthew T Mellon. He impressed everyone present by recalling his boyhood conversations with his great-grandfather Judge Thomas Mellon, who would tell tales of the miseries of the three-month Atlantic crossing he had endured way back in 1818.

> **WATER WEARY**
> People who lived in old-time rural Ireland say that one of the toughest aspects of life was having to ration the water, which had to be carried so laboriously from spring or well to the house.

Leaving for the New World

Particularly poignant is the indoor reconstruction of a 19th-century Ulster street, complete with post office, draper, saddler, ropemaker, pawnbroker and chemist. The dockside booking office leads to a gangplank into the gloomy hold of an emigrant ship, where the imagination

Demonstration of cottage handicrafts

soon re-creates the experience of the passengers, as they pitched westward across the Atlantic in such a dark, cramped, stinking, noisy hellhole.

The **American section** includes the primitive cabin of a Midwest settler, a smoke house and barn, and a Pennsylvania farmhouse, all built of logs. Both Old and New World collections are brought to life by costumed guides who inform and entertain while they carry out their tasks, such as baking and keeping sweet-scented turf fires burning.

A log house typical of those built by early Irish-American settlers in the wild Midwest

TAKING A BREAK

There is a café in the visitor centre serving meals and snacks.

✚ 196 C4　✉ Mellon Road, Castletown, Omagh, Co Tyrone　☎ 028 8224 3292; www.folkpark.com　🕔 Mar–Sep Tue–Sun 10–5; Oct–Feb Tue–Fri 10–4, Sat–Sun 11–4 (last admission 90 mins before closing)　💷 Moderate

ULSTER AMERICAN FOLK PARK: INSIDE INFO

Top tips　The Mellon Homestead and the ship and Dockside Gallery are two of the park's most popular sites. For the former, keep ahead as you leave the Information Centre, then bear right; for the latter, bear left from the Centre.

■ Forget your diet, and try any goodies that the guides may offer you: they are all freshly made on site.

Hidden gem　Don't overlook the **raised viewpoint** behind the Mellon Homestead. From here you get an excellent view over the whole park, with roofs peeping charmingly out of the trees.

4 Lough Erne and Belleek Pottery

One-third of County Fermanagh is under water. The centre of the county is entirely filled by the island-dotted waters of Upper and Lower Lough Erne. You can follow winding lanes along the shores in a car, on foot or by bicycle. Alternatively, you could rent a cruiser at Belleek, and spend a couple of days drifting lazily among more than 200 islands and their tangled backwaters – a wonderfully relaxing way to see Fermanagh. Now that the Victoria Canal linking Upper Lough Erne with the River Shannon has been reopened, you could actually cruise 480km (300 miles) from Belleek to Killaloe, in sheltered water all the way.

Fine China

Belleek and its celebrated pottery stands at the seaward end of the Lower Lough Erne. They have been making gleaming basket-weave pottery at **Belleek Pottery** since 1857, and in much the same way, with traditional tools made by the workers themselves. Wander around the factory and watch the craftspeople teasing the raw material – Cornish china clay and glass – into long snakes, then painstakingly constructing the delicate bowls and plates of latticework that will be decorated with tiny, handmade china flowers and painted to perfection. Of course you can buy a piece if you want, after the tour.

A craftsman at work at the Belleek Pottery

The calm waters of Lough Erne

The Lough and its Islands

Once legend says, Fermanagh was a dry plain, with a fairy well that was always kept covered. Two lovers, hastening to elope, drank at the well and forgot to replace the cover. As the first rays of sun touched the water it overflowed, and went on flowing until it had formed Lough Erne.

The county town of **Enniskillen**, with its 15th century castle nad Victorian park, sits on an island in the narrow waist between Upper and Lower Lough Erne. This is a great spot to base yourself when you explore the lough and its islands. Apart from their beauty, visitors are attracted by the little islands' extraordinary wealth of relics of the past, both Christian and pre-Christian. **Devenish Island** is reached by ferry (Apr–Sep) from Trory Point just downstream of Enniskillen. On Devenish you'll find the ruins of a 13th-century parish church, a fine carved high cross, the beautiful shell of St Mary's Priory (1449), and a very well preserved round tower dating from about 1160. From the tower's uppermost window, 25m (82 feet) up, you can enjoy great views over the lough and islands. A small museum explains the layout and history of this monastic site, founded during the sixth century by St Molaise, "Little Flame the Beautiful from multitudinous Devenish". This island is very peaceful, with its own special magic.

A different aura of pre-Christian enchantment hangs round the old cemetery at Caldragh on **Boa Island**, which can be reached by bridge from the north shore of Lower Lough Erne. Here you'll find a much-photographed pagan "Janus figure", dating perhaps from the fifth to the sixth century AD, with two faces looking in opposite directions, and a hollow in the "skull" between

TOUGH GUY

The story is told that when Belleek Pottery was being built, a construction worker fell from the roof to the ground, miraculously landing on his feet. He swallowed a glass of whiskey and was sent straight back up again to carry on with the job.

them that some experts have speculated might have been made to hold ceremonial blood.

On **White Island**, reached by a ferry from Castle Archdale marina, are still more enigmatic figures: seven stone statues more than a thousand years old, built side by side into a wall that was possible part of an older monastery. One holds a priest's bell and crosier; one has his hand on his chin; another is a *sheela-na gig* – a cross-legged woman in a sexually blatant attitude. These may signify the Seven Deadly Sins, but no one knows for sure…

TAKING A BREAK

You'll find simple, tasty sustenance such as casseroles with baked potatoes, quiches and salads at the **Belleek Pottery Tea Rooms** (tel: 028 6865 9300). For Enniskillen's best music and hospitality, visit **Blake's Of The Hollow** (tel: 028 6632 2143), a wonderful pub in a dip of the main street.

Enigmatic Janus figure on Boa Island

"JANUS" BY HEANEY

God-eyed, sex-mouthed, its brain
A watery wound…
Nobel Prize-winning poet Seamus Heaney responds to the Janus figure on Boa Island.

Belleek Pottery

✚ 196 A3 ✉ Belleek Pottery Visitors' Centre, Belleek, Co Fermanagh
☎ 028 6865 9300; www.belleek.ie ⏲ Jan–Feb Mon–Fri 9–5:30; Mar–Jun 9–5:30, Sat 10–5:30, Sun 2–5:30; Jul–Oct Mon–Sat 9–6, Sun 12–6; Nov–Dec 9–5:30, Sat 10–5:30 🎟 Moderate

Lough Erne

✚ 196 B3 ✉ Lough Erne information: Tourist Office, Wellington Road, Enniskillen, Co Fermanagh ☎ 028 6632 3110; www.fermanaghlakelands.com

LOUGH ERNE: INSIDE INFO

Top tip If you have to select just one of Lough Erne's islands, go for **Devenish Island**: the ecclesiastical remains there are stunning.

Hidden gem Take binoculars to Devenish Island, to see what most visitors miss: the **four stone heads** looking out from under the cap of the round tower.

At Your Leisure

5 Old Bushmills Distillery

Some of Ireland's best malt and blended whiskey is made here in the world's oldest licensed distillery (1608), housed in an attractive huddle of whitewashed buildings in the shadow of two pagoda towers.

The tour takes you around big copper tuns full of steaming mash, swan-shaped pot stills, and a warehouse where wooden kegs give off the smell of the evaporating "angels' share". In the shop you can buy Original or Black Bush blends, or classic malts.

➕ 197 D5 ✉ Bushmills, Co Antrim ☎ 028 2073 3218; www.bushmills.com 🕐 Tours: summer Mon–Fri 9:3–4:30, Sat Sun 11:30–4:30; winter Mon–Fri 9:30–3:30, Sat Sun 12:30–3:30. Tours run approximately every half hour and cannot be booked in advance 💷 Moderate

6 Downhill

This is as eccentric and fascinating a cluster of buildings as you'll find in all of Ireland. Now in the care of the National Trust, and connected by scenic footpaths, they were built on the cliff tops just west of Castlerock by a highly idiosyncratic Bishop of Londonderry.

The **Mussenden Temple** is perched precariously on the cliff edge. It is a classical rotunda, built 1783–85 by Frederick Hervey, 4th Earl of Bristol and Bishop of Londonderry, perhaps to accommodate one of his mistresses. Inland stands the roofless, gaunt ruin of **Downhill House**, the Bishop's country seat, and nearby are a beautiful and sheltered walled garden, a dovecote and an icehouse. The **Lion Gate** is topped with one of Hervey's armorial leopards.

➕ 197 D5 ✉ Mussenden Road, Castlerock, Co Londonderry ☎ 028 2073 1582; www.nationaltrust.org.uk 🕐 Temple: end Mar–early Oct daily 10–5. Grounds: all year daily dawn–dusk 💷 Inexpensive; parking moderate when Temple open

The Mussenden Temple at Downhill

The "Hands across the divide" peace statue in Derry

7 Londonderry/Derry

Known as Londonderry to loyalists, and Derry – from its original Irish name, Doire, meaning place of the oak trees, given to it by St Columba when he founded an abbey here – to nationalists, this walled city has been split by politics. Its streets saw major disturbances in the 1970s, but it has emerged as a forward-thinking city. The main attraction is the walk around the 17th-century city walls (➤ 181–183), but there are plenty of other things to enjoy, including the **Tower Museum**, with exhibitions covering the Armada and The Story of Derry; a looming 19th-century **Guildhall** (➤ 183); **St Columb's Cathedral** with relics of the epic siege of 1688–89, when the Protestant citizens defied the army of Catholic James II (➤ 182);

POLITICAL POT

In the Countess's Bedroom at Florence Court the chamber pot is of finest Belleek china. Strategically placed at the bottom is a portrait of 19th-century British prime minister William Gladstone, unpopular with the ruling Anglo-Irish classes because of his support for Home Rule and land reform.

and a **Craft Village** where shops and eateries cluster in the heart of the city.
➕ 196 C4

Tourist Information Centre
✉ 44 Foyle Street ☎ 028 7126 7284; www.discovernorthernireland.com 🚌 Foyle Street 🚊 Waterside Station, Duke Street

Tower Museum
✉ Union Hall Place ☎ 028 7137 2411; www.derrycity.gov.uk/museums 🕐 Tue–Sat 10–5 💷 Moderate

Guildhall
☎ 028 7137 7335 to arrange a tour (summer only); www.discovernorthernireland.com 🕐 Mon–Fri 9–5 💷 Free

8 Sperrin Mountains

In the An Creagán Heritage Centre you can learn about geology, local history, wildlife and folklore; you can even pan for gold in the nearby stream. All good stuff – but it's better still to get out and explore this wild range of hills that straddles the Tyrone/Derry border. Even the highest peak (Sawel, at 683m/2,240 feet) is easily climbed with good walking shoes; golden plover, raven, peregrine and red grouse breed on the moors; and twisting roads soon put you deep into unfrequented back country.
➕ 196 C4 ✉ An Creagán Heritage Centre, 274 Glenelly Road, Cranagh, Co Tyrone ☎ 028 8164 8142; www.an-creagan.com 🕐 Daily 11–5:30 💷 Free

9 Marble Arch Caves

The entrance to this system of semi-flooded caves lies about 8km (5 miles) due west of Florence Court. You can walk much of the system, and boats carry you the rest of the way, through caverns and chambers with glistening mineral walls and plenty of stalactites. Phone before visiting, as the caves can be closed for safety after heavy rain.

➕ 196 B3 ✉ Marlbank Scenic Loop, Florence Court, Enniskillen, Co Fermanagh ☎ 028 6634 8855; www.marblearchcaves.net 🕐 Jul–Aug daily 10–5; mid–Mar to Jun, Sep 10–4.30 💷 Expensive

10 Florence Court

A few kilometres southwest of Enniskillen, the big square central block and arcaded wings of Florence Court look out over immaculate gardens and parkland. This mid-18th-century house was gutted by fire in 1955, but has been superbly restored by the National Trust. Rich plasterwork in the hall, on the dining room ceiling and above the staircase is notable; as are the portraits of the Earls of Enniskillen with their red hair and imperious eagle noses. There's a fine cutaway scale model of the basement in Florence Court. In 2005 a thief stole a valuable 1950s cigarette case from the property but, apparently wracked with guilt, he

The Palladian mansion of Florence Court, former seat of the Earls of Enniskillen

OFF THE BEATEN TRACK
If you have a little more time to spare, take half a day to drive south of Armagh City through the lanes of South Armagh. This pretty area of tumbled small hills and quiet farming villages was branded "Bandit Country" by the world's media during 25 years of the Troubles. This Republican area of the province has been almost entirely neglected by the tourist industry, but its people are as friendly as anywhere else in Ireland, and steeped in traditions of story-telling and music-making.

returned it anonymously at the end of 2009.

➕ 196 B3 ✉ Florence Court, Enniskillen, Co Fermanagh ☎ 028 6634 8249; www.nationaltrust.org.uk 🏠 House: mid Mar to mid–Apr, Oct Sat–Sun 11–5; Easter hols, Jul–Aug daily 11–5; May–Jun, Sep, Mon, Wed–Sun 11–5. Grounds: end Feb to Easter daily 10–6; Easter–Oct 10–8; Nov–Jan 10–4 💷 Moderate

11 Castle Coole

Designed between 1790 and 1798 by James Wyatt, this is Ireland's finest neo-classical mansion. Behind the giant portico of this National Trust property lie superb furnishings, Irish oak floors and silk-hung state rooms. In the library, note the camels' heads on the gilt curtain pole, installed to celebrate Admiral Nelson's victory over Napoleon at the Battle of the Nile in 1798. As you go around, the guide will tell you the sad story of the 1st Earl of Belmore, whose wife ran off and left him desolate and alone in this huge house.

➕ 196 B3 ✉ Enniskillen, Co Fermanagh ☎ 028 6632 2690; www.nationaltrust.org.uk 🏠 House: Jul–Aug daily 12–6; Jun Mon–Wed, Fri–Sun 1–6; mid–Mar to May, Sep Sat–Sun and public hols 1–6. Grounds: Mar–Oct daily 10–7; Nov–Feb 10–4 💷 Moderate

12 Navan Centre and Fort

The Lords of ancient Ulster ruled from the Hill of Navan, just outside Armagh City, from c700BC to the

The ancient hill fort on Navan was once the capital of Ulster

fourth century AD. Misty figures of legend – bold King Conor's Knights of the Red Branch, the Ulster hero Cuchulainn and his arch-foe Queen Mebh of Connacht, beautiful Deirdre of the Sorrows – walk the domed green hill.

Beneath the turf lies an extraordinary structure built by Iron Age tribespeople: a vast mound of pebbles packed inside a gigantic timber hall, which the builders then deliberately burned down.

Start your visit at the Navan Centre below, where a short film, audio tour and interactive exhibition draws you into themyth, history and geology of the site. When you're saturated with information, a guide leads you to the fort, a five-minute walk from the centre.

➕ 197 D3 ✉ 81 Killylea Road, Armagh
☎ 028 3752 9644; www.visitarmagh.com
🕐 Site: open access; Centre: Jul–Sep daily 10–7; Oct–Dec 10–4 💷 Site: free; Centre: moderate

⑬ Saint Patrick's Trian

This unique visitor complex, in the heart of Armagh, features three major exhibitions: The Armagh Story, a visit to the city's past; Patrick's Testament, The Book of Armagh, featuring one of the greatest treasures to survive from Early Christian Ireland; and the Land of Lilliput, the story of Jonathan Swift's most famous work *Gulliver's Travels*.

The adventures are narrated with the help of a 6m (20ft) giant. The word *trian* derives from the ancient division of Armagh into three distinct districts.

➕ 197 D3 ✉ 40 English Street, Armagh
☎ 028 3752 1801; www.visitarmagh.com
🕐 Mon–Sat 10–5, Sun 2–5 💷 Moderate

⑭ Mountains of Mourne

The beautiful Mountains of Mourne fill Northern Ireland's southeast corner. Their conical profiles give the impression of mountains, but at an average height of just over 600m (1,968 feet), these are really tall fells. They offer wonderful walking and backroad exploring. The ascent of Slieve Donard, Northern Ireland's highest peak, is the most popular walk. Start from Donard Park, Newcastle, and follow the well-worn path through Donard Wood and the Glen River Valley to the summit. Allow around five hours.

The A2 coast road skirts the mountains from Newcastle, the area's main tourist centre and seaside resort, to Rostrevor, and there are numerous side lanes that can lead you up to the reservoir lakes of Silent Valley and over by Spelga Dam in wild scenery.

At the Mourne Heritage Trust in Newcastle, you can buy a pack of ten laminated cards that detail walks ranging from easy to strenuous.

➕ 197 E2 ✉ Mourne Heritage Trust, 87 Central Promenade, Newcastle, Co Down
☎ 028 4372 4059; www.mournelive.com
🕐 Mon–Fri 9–5

Where to...
Eat and Drink

Prices

Expect to pay per person for a meal excluding drinks and service

£ under £12   ££ £12–£24   £££ over £24

BELFAST

Beatrice Kennedy ££–£££

Located in a quiet, modest house in the University district, this restaurant has become one of the mainstays of Belfast cuisine, and is just the place for quiet, relaxing dining. Local seasonal produce tops the regularly changing menu, which can include starters of scallops and black pudding and mains of haddock and mash with chowder sauce, crispy belly of pork or rich towers of venison. Booking is essential.

197 E3 ⊠ 44 University Road, Belfast BT7 1N. ☎ 028 9020 2290; www. beatricekennedy.co.uk ⓦ Tue–Sat 5–10.30; Sun 12:30–2:30, 5–8

Crown Liquor Saloon £–££

Belfast's best-known pub (▶150), this former Victorian gin palace is now owned by the National Trust. A visit to one of its snugs (booths) to sample a thirst-quenching pint and half a dozen oysters served on crushed ice, or a bowl of steaming, tasty Irish stew, should be on your schedule. The Britannia Lounge upstairs, built with timbers

from the SS *Britannic* (sister ship to the *Titanic*), is worth a look.

137 E3 ⊠ 46 Great Victoria Street, Belfast BT2 7BA ☎ 028 9024 3187; www.crownbar.com ⓦ Flanigan's Bar and eatery: Mon–Sat 11–9

Made in Belfast £

Despite the name, the owners brought their glitzy grunge straight from the hip former home in Hoxton, London. With an eclectic mish mash of furniture, mirrors, odd ends of wallpaper, graffiti and mismatched lighting, they have created an unpretentious feel that is equalled by the food. You can choose salads with smoked mackerel or clonakilty black pudding, bacon and eggs, or opt for real comfort food like bangers and mash, pies, roast chicken or even a good old fish finger sandwich with chips.

197 E3 ⊠ 4 Wellington Street, Belfast BT1 6HT ☎ 028 9024 6712; www.madeinbelfastni. com ⓦ Lunch daily 12–3:30. Dinner: Sun–Tue 6–9, Wed–Thu 5–9:30, Fri–Sat 6–10

Mourne Seafood Bar ££–£££

Following its successful parent restaurant in Dundrum café in Newcastle, this has become an unmissable treat for fish fiends. Start with oysters or mussels in white wine from the establishment's own beds, and follow with seafood linguine, horseradish-crusted salmon or a white lemon sole. Accompany with white wine or specially brewed Mourne stout.

197 E3 ⊠ 34–36 Bank Street, Belfast BT1 1HL ☎ 028 9024 8544; www. mourneseafood.com ⓦ Tue–Thu noon–9:30, Fri–Sat 12–4, 5–10:30, Sun 1–6, Mon 12–5

Shu ££–£££

South Belfast's most popular brasserie-style restaurant is on the cosmopolitan Lisburn Road. Opened in 2000, it has gone on to receive many accolades for its service and eclectic menu. Salmon, pigeon, hake and much more, all served with divine sauces, plus rich desserts to die for. The set menu (Mon–Thu in the main restaurant)

Where to...
Stay

Prices
Expect to pay per night for a double room
£ under £60   **££** £60–£100   **£££** over £100

BELFAST

The Merchant Hotel £££

This hotel has become *the* grand hotel in Belfast, a Victorian former bank transformed into a luxury city centre retreat, complete with high ceilings, columns and gilt cornices. You can come for afternoon tea or dinner in The Great Room restaurant, but what everyone really wants to do is stay in one of the 26 bedrooms, which are spacious with rich textiles and marble bathrooms.

➕ 197 E3 ✉ 35–39 Waring Street, Belfast BT1 2DY ☎ 028 9023 4888; www. themerchanthotel.com

Tara Lodge ££

This stylish modern hotel has 18 rooms and a friendly, intimate atmosphere. An advantage is the secure parking – rare so close to the city centre. Each of the comfortable bedrooms has a bathroom, and facilities include satellite TV, Internet access and beverages.

➕ 197 E3 ✉ 36 Cromwell Road, Botanic Avenue, Belfast BT7 1JW ☎ 028 9059 0900; www.taralodge.com

Malone Lodge Hotel ££

The Malone Lodge is a friendly town house hotel, close to the University and the Ulster Museum.

is good value. Downstairs is a cocktail bar and bistro with DJs on Fridays and Saturdays.

➕ 197 E3 ✉ 253 Lisburn Road, Belfast BT9 7EN ☎ 028 9038 1655; www.shu-restaurant. com ⏰ Mon–Sat 12–2:30, 6–10 (bar till late)

THE ANTRIM COAST

The Cellar Restaurant ££

Located halfway along the Causeway coast, this central Ballycastle eatery makes a good stop-off. You can expect simply cooked fish and seafood, along with steaks, duck, lamb and chicken. Look out for specials like Ballycastle lobster and smoked cod.

➕ 197 E5 ✉ 11b The Diamond, Ballycastle, Co Antrim ☎ 028 2076 3037; www. thecellarrestaurant.co.uk ⏰ Mon–Fri 5–8:30 (9.30 in summer), Sat 12–8:30

Ramore Restaurant £–££

This family favourite offers easy eating with harbour views. Chunky homemade burgers, fish and chips and tobacco onions all feature on

the menu, alongside popular dishes like curry and lasagne. There are daily specials, good vegetarian options and a teatime menu for early bird diners.

➕ 197 D5 ✉ The Harbour, Portrush, Co Antrim ☎ 028 7082 4313; www. ramorerestaurant.com ⏰ Mon–Thu 12:15–2:15, 5–10, Fri 12:15–2:15, 5–10:30, Sat 12:15–2:15, 4:45–10:30, Sun 12:30–3, 5–9

MOUNTAINS OF MOURNE

The Buck's Head ££

This attractive restaurant/bar has a conservatory at the back and a garden for fine weather, with views of Dundrum Bay from the top. Good food and service plus long opening hours make this the place to stop on a tour. Local produce, especially seafood from Dundrum Bay, is prominent and there's always imaginative vegetarian food.

➕ 197 E3 ✉ 77 Main Street, Dundrum, Co Down ☎ 028 4375 1868 ⏰ Daily 12–2:30, 5–6:30, 7–9

Macklins Bar and the highly rated Green Door restaurant offer a range of eating options too.

197 E3 ✉ **60 Eglantine Avenue, Malone Road, Belfast BT9 6DY** ☎ **028 9038 8060; www.malonelodgehotelbelfast.com**

ENNISKILLEN

Abocurragh Farm Guesthouse £–££

This lovely bed-and-breakfast is on a working dairy farm in a very beautiful part of Fermanagh. Spacious bedrooms have wonderful views, and there are facilities for children, such as special meals and a babysitting service.

196 B3 ✉ **Letterbreen, Enniskillen, Co Fermanagh BT74 9AG** ☎ **028 6634 8484; www.abocurragh.com**

THE ANTRIM COAST

Bushmills Inn ££

Thoughtful development has added to the appeal of this well-run 19th-century coaching inn near the Giants Causeway. A surf fire and traditional furniture in the hall set the tone, and public rooms are all in keeping with the country theme. Bedrooms are furnished in a comfortable cottage style, and even the new bathrooms seem to belong to an earlier era. There is a Taste of Ulster restaurant and a gas-lit bar.

197 D5 ✉ **9 Dunluce Road, Bushmills, Co Antrim BT57 8QG** ☎ **028 2073 3300; www.bushmillsinn.com**

LONDONDERRY/DERRY

Beech Hill Country House Hotel £££

Just outside the city walls, this 18th-century house has retained many original details. Bedrooms vary in size and outlook but all have bath or shower rooms and are furnished with antiques. The bar is popular, and serves good food. Gym, jacuzzi and sauna, massage and aromatherapy steam room.

196 C4 ✉ **32 Ardmore Road, Derry BT47 3QP** ☎ **028 7134 9279; www.beech-hill.com**

Greenhill House £

This Georgian farmhouse nestles in well-tended gardens with splendid views over open countryside. Bedrooms include two large family rooms; the bedrooms are not luxurious, but they have bathrooms and their furnishings make them far more comfortable than one might expect in farmhouse accommodation. Dinner is available for residents by prior arrangement.

197 D5 ✉ **24 Greenhill Road, Aghadowey, Co Londonderry BT51 4EU** ☎ **028 7086 8241; www.greenhill-house.co.uk** ⏱ **Closed Nov–early Mar**

DUNGANNON

Grange Lodge ££

The comfort and hospitality provided at this lovely Georgian house along with its location at the end of the M1 motorway make this a good base for touring. There are extensive grounds to explore, including 1ha (2.5 acres) of manicured gardens. Bedrooms (and bathrooms) are very comfortable and the food (residents' dinner and breakfast) is superb.

197 D3 ✉ **7 Grange Road, Dungannon, Co Tyrone BT71 1EJ** ☎ **028 8778 4212; www.grangelodgecountryhouse.com** ⏱ **Closed 13 Dec–1 Feb**

MOUNTAINS OF MOURNE

Hastings Slieve Donard Hotel £££

This prestigious Victorian hotel, part of the Hastings chain, stands in grounds beneath the Mountains of Mourne and beside the Royal County Down Golf Links. Renovated in the late 1990s, the accommodation is furnished to a high standard, and every bathroom sports a yellow Hastings duck! There's a health club, and Tollymore Forest Park provides excellent walking.

197 E3 ✉ **Downs Road, Newcastle, Co Down BT33 0AH** ☎ **028 4372 1066; www.hastingshotels.com**

Where to...
Shop

The North, with its long tradition of craftsmanship, is the best part of Ireland for linen, handmade lace and parian china. Look for beautifully made woollen goods and hand-cut Tyrone crystal.

BELFAST

Belfast's main shopping area is around Donegall Place, High Street and Royal Avenue; **Victoria Square** (between Ann and Chichester streets) is Belfast's top shopping centre. **The Wicker Man** (44–46 High Street, tel: 028 9024 3550) stocks the craftwork from all over Ireland. **Smyth's Irish Linens** (65 Royal Avenue, tel: 028 9024 2786) has beautiful linen goods, and **Smyth & Gibson** (Bedford House, Bedford Street, tel: 028 9023 0388) sells luxurious linen shirts and accessories. **St George's Market** (May Street) opens on Fridays (6am–1pm), with stalls selling everything from antiques to vegetables. On Saturday there's a food market here (9am–3pm), where you can buy fish, cheese and continental produce.

LONDONDERRY/DERRY

In Derry, **The Donegal Shop** (Shipquay Street, tel: 028 7126 6928) does great linen, tweeds and knitwear, and the **Derry Craft Village** (off Shipquay Street, tel: 028 7126 0329) has craft demonstrations. **Austins** (2 The Diamond, tel: 028 7126 1817) is a department store stocking a wide range of high-quality local goods.

Where to...
Be Entertained

The Arts Council of Northern Ireland (tel: 028 9038 5200) **produces the monthly** *Artslink*. **More information is available at tourist information offices and at www.culturenorthernireland.org.**

SPORT

In addition to the usual sporting pursuits of greyhound racing, horse racing, soccer, rugby and cricket, the Northern Irish love watching and participating in their native sports, principally hurling and Gaelic football. In Armagh you might see "bullets" being played, which basically involves hurling metal balls along country lanes. Other activities include golf, cycling, fishing, walking and horse riding. Details on all these and other options are available from tourist information offices.

MUSIC

There's plenty of informal music in Northern Ireland. In Belfast, good places to experience traditional music are **The John Hewitt Bar** (51 Donegall Street, tel: 028 9023 3768) and **The Spaniard** (3 Skipper Street, tel: 028 9023 2448). **The Kitchen Bar** (36–40 Victoria Square, tel: 028 9032 4901) has music on Friday nights. Club fashions move fast, but Botanic attracts a lively young crowds at the **Limelight** and **Spring & Airbrake** (both on Ormeau Avenue). The **Odyssey** (Queen's Quay) is Belfast's biggest venue, hosting everything from top rock bands to wrestling.

Walks and Tours

1 HILL OF HOWTH

Walk

This delightful walk is a favourite weekend stroll of Dubliners. It is easily reached by train, crosses varied terrain from hill slopes to coastal paths, and has tremendous views over the city, Dublin Bay and the coast and hills for 50km (30 miles) around. It makes an ideal change of pace when you are feeling jaded with central Dublin and long to get some fresh sea air into your lungs.

DISTANCE 11km (7 miles) **TIME** 3 hours (4 if you stop…and you should) **START/END POINT** Howth DART railway station (24 minutes from Connolly Station in central Dublin). For information tel: 01 836 6222 ✚ 201 E5

medieval Europe. There's a great view here over the packed white houses of Howth to the crooked crab-claws of the harbour breakwaters. Howth has long been a favoured dwelling place for writers, Trinity College

dons, poets and artists, and more recently for well-heeled commuters who want to live conveniently close to, but not actually in, Ireland's capital city.

1–2

Turn left out of the DART station in Howth to pass the **harbour**. This was where Erskine Childers, author of the classic spy thriller *The Riddle of the Sands*, landed guns and ammunition from his little yacht *Asgard* in July 1914 to help foment a nationalist uprising.

2–3

In a few hundred metres turn right up Abbey Street. Beside Ye Olde Abbey Tavern climb the steps on the right to reach the ruins of the **abbey** – a seat of learning famed throughout

3–4

Turn down Church Street into Abbey Street, and then next right up St Lawrence's Road. In 100m (110 yards) keep going along Grace O'Malley Road, then turn left up Grace O'Malley Drive. At the third bend veer right onto a short path beside woodland, leading to a road; go ahead for 20m (22 yards), then right up steps.

4–5

Turn right at the top, and ascend a ramp beside house No 53 ("Ballylinn"). Keep ahead up a grassy slope, go through trees until you emerge in front of a steep bank with a football pitch on top. Follow the track round to the right, then left, keeping the bank to your left and the golf course to your right.

5–6
The track bends to the left at the top of the golf course; follow the path into the trees, across the aptly named Bog of Frogs, and on under the crags of Dun Hill. Cross the golf course and climb the steep heathery slope

From the ruins of 11th-century Howth Abbey there is a splendid view out across the harbour to the rocky island of Ireland's Eye

ahead (red-and-white striped poles) on a rough path that leads to the top of Shielmartin. Take time up here to admire the superb views across Dublin Bay and the city to the Wicklow Hills. Knobby, white quartzite boulders form a ring round the crown of **Shielmartin**. They were placed here 2,000 years ago to mark the burial place of an Irish warrior king, Crimhthan Niadhnair. Helped by his wife, Nar of the Brugh (some say she was a

goddess), he became rich beyond dreams of avarice by making frequent raids across the Irish Sea to plunder the Romans who had newly arrived in Britain. Whether his golden treasure is buried on Shielmartin is open to romantic speculation.

6–7
A clear path leads off the summit, steeply down to Carrickbrack Road. Turn left; in 300m (330 yards) cross the road, go through a swing gate ("Dangerous Cliffs" sign – but don't be alarmed!) and take the path down to the shore.

7–8
Here you turn left and follow the narrow but well-defined coastal path for 8km (5 miles), past the Baily Lighthouse on its promontory and all the way round Howth Head and back to the DART station where your walk started.

TAKING A BREAK
There are many pubs and restaurants in Howth. Try Abbey Tavern in Abbey Street (tel: 01 839 0307) for delicious fish and an excellent pint of stout.

2 LIMERICK HIGHLIGHTS

Walk

Limerick's city centre is well worth a visit, being home to the elegant Newtown Pery area of Georgian buildings and King's Island, across an estuary of the River Shannon, where King John built a castle.

DISTANCE 3km (2 miles) TIME 3–6 hours depending on stops
START POINT Tourist Information Centre, Arthur's Quay Park END POINT King John's Castle ✚ 199 E4

1–2

The best place to start is at the Tourist Information Centre beside the Shannon in Arthur's Quay Park. From here walk straight ahead along **Henry Street**. As you pass Shannon Street, notice the two large Georgian buildings on the right-hand side. Plaques indicate that these were the homes of William Pery, Bishop of Limerick, and his brother, Edmund Sexton Pery, who instigated the building of Georgian Limerick, now known as Newtown Pery.

2–3

Although some of the buildings were demolished, the district spreads about six blocks in each direction. Walk ahead, zigzagging your way along Cecil Street, O'Connell Street and Mallow Street to take in the fine Georgian architecture until you reach the **People's Park**, a green oasis filled with hawthorn, ash, horse chestnut, oak and other trees. Georgian buildings surround the park but the western side holds the most interest; **No 1 Pery Square**, a luxury boutique hotel comprising six immaculately restored Georgian houses ▶ 117); and the **Georgian House & Garden**, at No 2, a restored museum-house open to the public and complete with period furnishings and artefacts donated by the Pery and Carroll families.

3–4

Go left from the park along Pery Street and head back to O'Connell Street, which becomes

THE PERY FAMILY

The Perys have played an important role in the history of Limerick since Edmund Sexton Pery (1719–1806) built the Georgian area of the town. While he was an Irish parliamentarian and 1st (and last) Viscount of Newtown Pery, his brother was the Protestant Bishop of Limerick and 1st Baron of Glentworth. His son, Edmund Henry Pery, became the 1st Earl of Limerick, a title that continues today – Edmund Christpher Pery (b1963) is the current and 7th Earl. They are also related to Aubrey de Vere (1814–1902), a renowned Limerick-born poet.

CASTLE ST

6 King John's Castle

NICHOLAS STREET

5 St Mary's Cathedral

MARY ST

George's Quay

BANK PL

BRIDGE ST

Mathew Bridge

Hunt Museum 4

TAKING A BREAK

Ducans Restaurant in the Hunt Museum has a prime position overlooking the Shannon. It's a good place to stop for drinks and snacks as well as hot meals.

PLACES TO VISIT

Georgian House & Garden
☎ 061 314130 ☉ Mon–Fri 10–4
💷 Inexpensive

Hunt Museum
☎ 061 312833; www.huntmuseum.com
☉ Mon–Sat 10–5, Sun 2–5 💷 Moderate

King John's Castle
☎ 061 711200 ☉ Daily 10–5 💷 Moderate

pedestrianised after Shannon Street and is bustling with shops, cafés and restaurants. Continue to the end where it becomes Rutland Street. On the left, before the bridge, is the **Hunt Museum**, which holds one of Ireland's finest artefact and art collections, from Neolithic archaeological finds to works by Picasso and Renoir.

4–5

Cross the bridge to King's Island and walk up Bridge Street to St Mary's Cathedral. Founded in the 12th century by the last king of Munster, Donal Mor O'Brien, the cathedral's most notable features are the ancient West Door, its 17th-century organ and the 14th-century tower, which has a peal of eight bells. Also look out for the Pery family vault to the left of the main door.

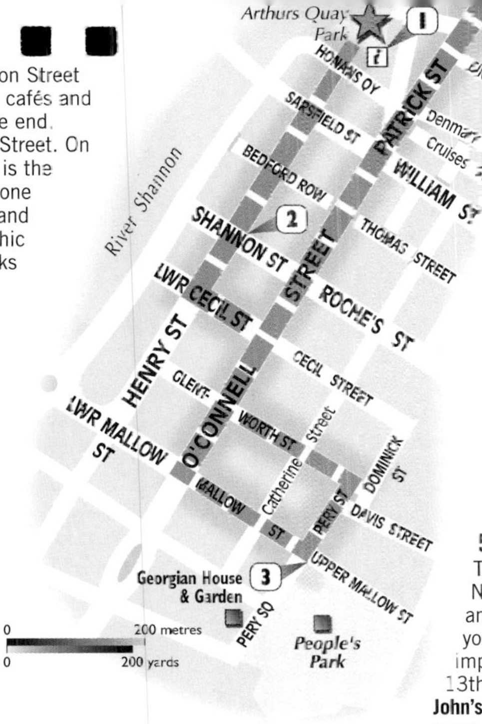

5–6

Turn left along Nicholas Street and at the end you'll come to the impressive 13th-century **King John's Castle**, which looms over the River Shannon. You can see its cylindrical towers from outside but go in to walk along the battlements with fine views over the city. To the left of the castle on Castle Land is the small, free **Limerick City Museum**, a treasure trove of photos, archaeological finds and Limerick lace. To the right of the castle is the former Bishop's Palace now home to the Limerick Civic Trust.

3 CROAGH PATRICK

Walk

The ascent of Croagh Patrick is one of Ireland's classic hill climbs. The climb itself is not technically challenging, although the second half is a stamina-sapping scramble up loose scree. The view from the summit – coast, islands and mountains – will take your breath away. Most visitors opt for the short climb from Murrisk, but the 37km (23-mile) longer and original pilgrimage route, beginning at Ballintober Abbey, repays the effort.

DISTANCE 7km (4 miles) up and down; ascent of 765m (2,510 feet) **TIME** 4–5 hours. Ancient Pilgrimage Route takes 2 days **START/END POINT** Murrisk, on R355 9km (5 miles) west of Westport, for the short route; Ballintober Abbey, 11km (7 miles) south of Castlebar, off the N84 Ballinrobe road, for the long route ⊞ 194 C2

Short Pilgrimage Route

1–2

Leave your car in the car park next to Owen Campbell's pub in Murrisk, opposite the moving Coffin Ship National Famine Memorial. The path begins at the back of the car park beside the Visitor Centre and stalls renting out walking sticks.

2–3

Walk past a statue of St Patrick where pilgrims often stop to pray and continue along the well-worn path that leads to the saddle at 500m (1,640 feet).

3–4

Take a deep breath and tackle the very steep slope to the summit. Return on the same path.

IRELAND'S HOLY MOUNTAIN

Croagh Patrick (or The Reek) is a place of pilgrimage and penance. Each year on Garland or Reek Sunday, the last Sunday in July, as many as 50,000 people (many of them barefoot), ranging in age from 8 to 80, climb the mountain and stop to pray at several mounds of stones en route as well as at the little chapel on the summit. St Patrick (▶ 14) is said to have climbed up Croagh Patrick's steep slopes in AD441, preaching from the summit and breaking the power of a cloud of demons by hurling his bell through them. He also begged successfully for deliverance of the souls of the Irish people on Doomsday, and banished all snakes from the island.

MAPS

If you are following 37km (23-mile) Tochar Phadraig from Ballintober Abbey, you will find these Irish OS 1:50,000 maps useful: 30, 31, 37, 38.

Climbing Croagh Patrick on Reek Sunday

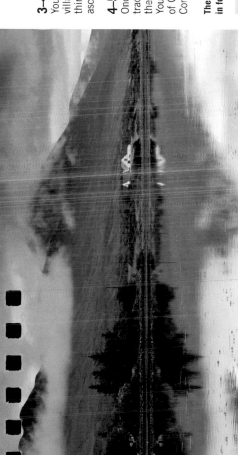

3-4

You can break your journey halfway at the village of Aghagower, or accomplish the whole thing in one go, but take into account the stiff ascent up loose scree that awaits you.

4-5

Once under The Reek itself, follow the track up the south flank to the saddle, then sweat up the rock slide to the summit. You'll be rewarded with spectacular views of Clew Bay and the Nephin Beg and Connemara mountains.

The mountain is often atmospherically swathed in fog

TAKING A BREAK

As you return to Murrisk, refreshed in spirit but leg-weary and footsore, stop at **Owen Campbell's** pub at the foot of the path. The pub is basic and doesn't smell the best, but the Guinness is superb and coming here for a pint is almost a rite of passage if you've just descended from Croagh Patrick. The interior of the pub is hung with photographs of Reek pilgrims.

Ancient Pilgrimage Route

1-2

A former chariot route that predates Christianity, this pilgrim path begins at St Patrick's Well in the grounds of Ballintubber Abbey (www.ballintubber.ie). Follow the marker stones incised with crosses. These will lead you along the field paths and lanes of St Patrick's Causeway, known in Irish as Tochar Phadraig.

2-3

The Tochar, an ancient pilgrim route, runs west for 37km (23 miles), aiming for the cone of Croagh Patrick. En route it passes holy wells, standing stones, monastic sites, prehistoric burial mounds and inscribed rocks.

4 YEATS COUNTRY

Drive

DISTANCE 160km (100 miles) **TIME** Half a day **START/END POINT** Sligo town **■** 195 E3

William Butler Yeats (1865–1939), winner of the 1923 Nobel Prize for Literature and arguably Ireland's greatest poet, had the flat-topped mountains and sea-beaten shores of County Sligo always in his mind. This beautiful and weathered countryside, where Yeats spent happy childhood months with his grandparents and cousins, inspired many of his best-known poems, and symbolised the mystery, strangeness and strength of his native land.

Most of the ragged circuit of this Yeats Country route is signposted by brown roadsigns showing a quill and inkstand.

1–2

Having first got into the mood by visiting the many W B Yeats sites in Sligo town (▶ 137), leave the town along Castle Street and make your way west towards the distinctive 328m (1,076-foot) mound of Knocknarea.

Just outside Sligo, a brown notice points left for **Carrowmore Tombs**. Sprawling across fields a couple of kilometres down this side

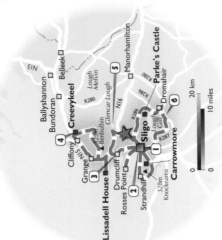

road is the largest concentration of megalithic monuments in Ireland – stone circles, dolmens and cairns, most of them now reduced to a few stones, largely as a result of quarrying, but one or two still nearly intact. It is a haunting place, which would be even more impressive were it not for the huge orange-hued riding centre that dominates this ancient site.

Back on the Sligo road, turn left to pass close under Knocknarea; a side road is signposted "Meascán Meadhba", and leads via a 45-minute walk to "**Queen Mebh's tomb**" and a wonderful 80km (50-mile) view. Mebh or Maeve was the first-century warrior queen of Connacht who initiated the "Cattle Raid of Cooley" (▶ 11). The big green cairn that stands out against the sky on the summit of Knocknarea, said to be her tomb, is in fact a passage grave, filled with 40,000 boulders, that predates Queen Mebh by at least 2,000 years.

The main road drops to an intersection; turn right here, and beside the Sancta Maria Hotel go left to reach the stony shore enormous grassy dunes and splendid hill views of Strandhill beach. The cliffs and domed brow of Knocknarea hang behind Strandhill, on whose shore W B Yeats saw and heard the Atlantic waves crash during storms:

"The wind has bundled up the clouds high over Knocknarea,

And thrown the thunder on the stones for all that Maeve can say."

2-3

Return into Sligo and take the N15 Bundoran–Lifford road north out of town. On the outskirts bear left on R291 to **Rosses Point**, a neat little seaside village with a really beautiful view over Sligo Bay and some fine sandy beach walks. Yeats and his brother used to spend happy summer holidays here.

Return to N15 and go north to **Drumcliff**. The stump of a round tower stands by the road, and a heavily carved high cross dating from about AD1000 forms part of the churchyard wall. But the focal point is W B Yeats's grave, next to the northwest corner of the tower. Yeats actually died in France, but his body was brought back to Ireland in 1948 and buried here as he

W B Yeats's tombstone, in Drumcliff churchyard

wished. A gravel walk leads to a plain limestone slab which is inscribed with last lines of the epitaph poem composed by Yeats for himself (see picture). The beginning of the poem is:

"Under bare Ben Bulben's head
In Drumcliff Churchyard Yeats is laid..."

And the view is just that: the simple gravestone, a line of trees, and Ben Bulben in the distance.

3-4

Continue 8km (5 miles) up N15, then bear left for **Lissadell House**, ancestral home of the Gore-Booth family. Two members of the family befriended Yeats. One was the poet Eva Gore-Booth; the other, her sister Constance, Countess Markievicz, played an active part in the 1916 Easter Rising. She was subsequently elected to Westminster as the first female Member of Parliament (though she never took her seat).

Return to N15 and turn left to continue through **Cliffony**, with Ben Bulben's profile

Horseback riding with **Ben Bulben** as a backdrop

changing from that of a lion couchant to a perfect flat-topped table. As you leave the village, look for the car park just before the intersection (signposted for Mullagmore); from here it's just a step to the well-signposted **Creevykeel court tomb**. This complicated cairn was built between 3000 and 2000BC with a central court and several burial chambers, all approached through massive stone portals. One even has its rugged lintel still in place.

4–5

Turn back along N15, and immediately right at the intersection (brown "Ballintrillick" sign) on a long, straight country road. Under Benwisken, cross a lane and follow "Gleniff Horseshoe" signs. **Gleniff** is a remote valley hemmed in by basalt crags, where sheep graze under huge fellsides rushing with waterfalls.

The great dark rock arch that hangs above the top end of Gleniff is said to be the bed of runaway lovers Diarmuid and Gráinne. Diarmuid had the bad luck to cross swords with the hero Fionn MacCumhaill, a former fiancé of Gráinne, and suffered the indignity of having his severed head sent to his true love by the implacable Fionn.

Back on the lane, turn left and continue for 8km (5 miles). Turn left on N15 for Sligo.

In 3.2km (2 miles) sidetrack left to **Glencar**, where you turn left and head along the north bank of Glencar Lough to view the fine waterfall in its wooded cleft. It is in full force after rain, but this is a beautiful spot in any weather.

5–6

Return to Glencar and continue straight onto N16, turning right towards Sligo. Take R286 for "Dromahair" signs, and also brown "Lough Gill" and "Parke's Castle" signs. You pass Colgagh Lough below, and are soon down on the wooded shore of **Lough Gill**, one of the most attractive stretches of water in County Sligo. Follow the road along the north shore of the lough. You pass the turreted 17th-century stately home of Parke's Castle, a picture of grim impregnability. Boat trips run from the inlet by the castle to the **Lake Isle of Innisfree**, subject of Yeats's best known poem, but you can reach the shore much nearer this tiny island by way of Dromahair. On the far edge of the village bear right (following the "Ballintogher/Sligo" sign); then after 1km (0.5 miles) take the first narrow lane on the right to wriggle down to the lake shore. Some 200m (220 yards) out lies the tree-smothered round blob of an islet whose peaceful beauty, pictured in the midst of city

bustle, brought great solace to Yeats:

"I will arise and go now, and go to Innisfree,
And a small cabin build there, of clay and wattles made:

Nine bean-rows will I have there, a hive for the honey-bee,

And live alone in the bee-loud glade..."

Yeats never did build his wattle cabin on Innisfree. But he truly loved this peaceful lake, and you can well appreciate why, as you complete the circuit of Lough Gill before returning to Sligo town on R287 and N4.

5 WALLS OF DERRY

Walk

This circuit of the city walls of Derry gives insight into the passion that divides society in Northern Ireland. The walls are most associated with the 105-day Siege of Derry in 1689 and with the sometimes contentious annual parades by the Apprentice Boys (► 182).

DISTANCE 1.6km ¹⁄₁ mile. **TIME** 2 hours
START/END POINT The Tower Museum, Union Hall Place, near Magazine Gate 🕀 196 C4

1–2

Walk into the old city through **Shipquay Gate**, and turn to your right to climb to the top of the walls by the Tower Museum in Union Hall Place. The walls of Derry, 6–8m (19–26 feet) tall and the same thickness, form a belt of solid stone that buckles the city into its high defensive position. They were built during 1613–18 by guilds from London that had taken over the running of the city and were determined to see it properly protected against all potential enemies – chiefly, local clans resistant to the rule of the British Crown. The walls created an enclave

based on a cross of streets that ran from a diamond-shaped central marketplace – The Diamond – to four great gates: Shipquay Gate (northwest), Butcher's Gate (northeast), Bishop's Gate (southwest) and Ferryquay Gate (southeast). Three more gates were added later.

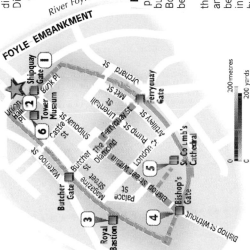

2–3

Set off southwest above **Magazine Street**, looking down on the tangled roofs of the walled city. Cross over **Castle Gate**, then **Butcher's Gate**. A little further along, pause on the **Royal Bastion**, a stout outward bulge, and look west across the roofs of the Bogside to the far-off hills of Donegal, a beautiful backdrop.

"You are now entering Free Derry," states the most renowned mural in the Bogside, while another depicts Bernadette Devlin, who at 21 became the youngest ever MP to be elected, in 1969. You can see several more murals by the Bogside artists, mainly along Rossville

Street, where much of the political trouble was focused over the years. Down on them frown the bastion cannon presented to the city in 1642. Up here stood Walker's Pillar, a great local landmark that offered wonderful wide views from the top until the IRA blew it up in 1973. The Apprentice Boys on their December marches would string up from the pillar an effigy of Robert Lundy, Governor of Derry during the Great Siege of 1688–89.

3–4

Walk on to **Bishop's Gate**, and climb down to admire the gate itself, rebuilt in classical style in 1789. Two local river gods, bearded and crowned with waterweeds, adorn its arch, Foyle looking out and Boyne looking into the city.

It was to Bishop's Gate that Britain's deposed Catholic King James II rode

Bearded river god, crowned with water weeds, on Bishop's Gate

on 18 April, 1689, to demand the surrender of 30,000 Protestants walled up inside Derry. The Great Siege began then; but the citizens of Derry had been locked in since the previous December, when the celebrated 13 Apprentice Boys seized the keys of the four gates and locked them against the Jacobite army.

4–5

Walk down Bishop Street Within, then right up St Columb Court, to reach **St Columb's Cathedral**, a veritable museum to the Great Siege. It was from the tower that the cry of "No Surrender!" was launched in response to King James's demands. Once Governor Robert Lundy had been ejected, the defenders found a champion in the formidable Reverend George Walker.

In the Chapter House are displayed the keys seized by the Apprentice Boys, brick cannon balls, and a portrait of George Walker in armour. In the church is a plaque to Captain Michael Browning, killed on 28 July, 1689, as his ship *Mountjoy* smashed through the boom built by the besiegers across the river, bringing relief supplies into the city. For 7,000 of the 30,000 defenders (who had eaten every dog, cat and rat in the place), it was too late. The cathedral's entrance hall contains a stand holding the "First Air Mail Letter", an iron mortar bomb which was fired into the city with the Jacobites' surrender demands sticking out of its fuse hole.

Don't leave St Columb's without enjoying some of its other treasures: ancient regimental flags, carved pew-ends, the great oak tabernacle over the Bishop's chair, and the beautiful late Victorian "Garden of Gethsemane" window.

5–6

Return to Bishop Street Within and continue down to The Diamond. Turn right along Ferryquay Street to rejoin the walls at Ferryquay Gate. Complete your circuit, to finish at the **Tower Museum**. The museum was built as an act of faith and optimism

MARTYRS' MOUND

Outside the east end of the cathedral is the Martyrs' Mound, a green burial hump where 4,500 victims of the Great Siege lie. They were interred there a century after the siege, having been exhumed from the city cellars in which they had been hastily buried during the emergency.

Symbol of ancient defiance: 17th-century cannon line Derry's city walls

at the height of the Troubles when over a quarter of the walled city's buildings had been destroyed. It has amply repaid the vision. This is an excellent museum, taking you by way of curving "time tunnels" into various phases of Derry's history. The Troubles are not shirked, but given even-handed treatment.

TAKING A BREAK

The **Dunloe Bar** (tel: 028 7126 7716) in Waterloo Street is a good place to stop for a light lunch, and there is sometimes live music to entertain you while you eat.

PLACES TO VISIT

Guildhall

Make sure you pop into the splendidly florid Victorian Guildhall. A bombing in 1972 destroyed the stained-glass windows, but by some miracle the original 19th-century watercolour designs had been preserved in London, and the windows were painstakingly reconstructed.

🕿 Mon–Fri 9–5　💷 Free

St Columb's Cathedral

🕿 028 7126 7313, www.stcolumbscathedral. org 🕙 Apr–Sep Mon–Sat 9–5; Oct–Mar Mon–Sat 9–1, 2–4　💷 Inexpensive

Tower Museum

🕿 028 7137 2411　🕙 Jul–Aug daily 10–4:30; Mar–Jun Mon–Sat 10–4:30; Sep–Feb Mon–Fri 10–4:30　💷 Moderate

6 STRANGFORD LOUGH

Drive

The 37km (23-mile) Ards Peninsula hangs down like an elephant's trunk east of Belfast. This narrow outpost of County Down shelters the great tidal inlet of Strangford Lough and all but encloses it. At its southern end, the ferry villages of Portaferry and Strangford face each other across a gap only 500m (550 yards) wide. Strangford Lough is home to millions of geese, ducks and wading birds: brent geese and arctic terns are two species that stop here on their annual migration. The peninsula's east coast, which faces out into the Irish Sea, has a run of huge sandy beaches interspersed with rocky coves. It's a beautiful place, unknown to most visitors to Ireland.

DISTANCE 160km (100 miles). This includes the 10-minute car ferry ride between Portaferry and Strangford (operates half-hourly) **TIME** 1 day **START/END POINT** Newtownards (on A20, 10km/6 miles east of Belfast)
✚ 197 F3

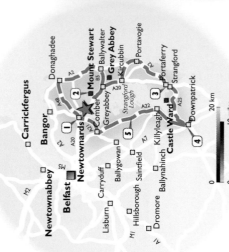

The ferry crosses Strangford Lough

1–2

Starting at **Newtownards** at the northern end of Strangford Lough, take A48 across the shoulder of the peninsula to the fishing village of Donaghadee, whose harbour was extended in the 1820s to cope with a flourishing ferry trade to Portpatrick in southwest Scotland.

Many famous people have stepped ashore or embarked at Donaghadee: among them are the poet John Keats, biographer James Boswell, composer Franz Liszt, writer Daniel Defoe, and Peter the Great, Tsar of Russia, who (locals will tell you) stayed at Grace Neill's pub in the High Street while touring Europe in 1697–98.

Follow A2 down the coast, admiring the fine beaches, to Ballywalter, where you strike inland along B5 to Greyabbey on the shore of Strangford Lough. There's the ruin of 12th-century **Grey Abbey** to explore here; then bear right up the A20 shore road to **Mount Stewart**. This splendid National Trust house, still lived in by a member of the Stewart family, feels warm and domestic notwithstanding the chandeliers and fine inlaid wood floors. Its gardens are among the National Trust's best, developed by Lady Londonderry from 1921 onwards in dashingly idiosyncratic style, and ornamented with weird stone sculptures of freakish beasts.

2–3

Return along A20 through Greyabbey and head on south, stopping now and then to get out the binoculars and admire the **bird**

life of Strangford Lough – godwit, redshank, curlew and plover, and in winter huge flocks of pale-bellied brent geese all the way from Greenland. At Kircubbin, weave your way back across the peninsula and continue your coast drive south through small fishing villages such as Ballyhalbert and Portavogie, renowned for its prawns and haddock.

When you reach Cloughey, you can either carry on south to the rugged tip of the peninsula at Ballyquintin Point, or cut back inland to Dorn on Strangford Lough, a nature reserve and another excellent birdwatching spot. Either way, aim to end up at the pretty little port of **Portaferry**, where you catch the car ferry over the narrows to Strangford.

Crossing the mouth of Strangford Lough, you enter what is known as "St Patrick's Country". Here Ireland's patron saint is said to have landed in AD432 on his mission to convert the Irish; and here in the abbey at the monastery of Saul he died in AD461. Spend a couple of hours cruising along the back roads of this quiet green landscape.

3–4

Follow A25 from Strangford to pass **Castle Ward**. The house, now a National Trust property, was built in 1762–68 by Bernard

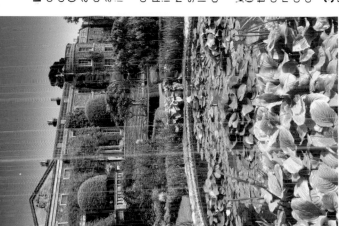

Water features are prominent in the beautifully kept gardens at Mount Stewart

Ward and his wife, Anne. He liked the Palladian style, she the romanticism; and both wanted their own way. So Castle Ward has a graceful Palladian front and some tastefully furnished classical rooms, while around the back are Moorish windows, pinnacles, and rooms with extravagant pointed door arches and elaborate plasterwork fan vaulting. As for the ill-matched couple, they eventually separated.

Continue along A25 into **Downpatrick**. On a mound outside the cathedral lies a giant slab inscribed "PATRIC". Does St Patrick lie under this stone together with Ireland's other two major-league saints, Brigid and Columb? Historians say no: folklorists and others say yes, and strew the slab with daffodils on St Patrick's Day. It's a lovely spot, whatever the truth.

4–5

Two or three kilometres (2 miles) southeast of Downpatrick, signposted off the Ardglass road, you'll find **Struell Wells**, a curious and peaceful spot where ancient stone bathhouses conceal ice-cold springs in which Patrick is said to have immersed himself.

Return to Downpatrick, from where A22 takes you back north to Newtownards up the west shore of Strangford Lough. Spare

time for a stroll along the waterside track at **Quoile Pondage National Nature Reserve** just outside Downpatrick, and be sure to detour out across the causeways to lonely little **Mahee Island**. Here you'll find a broken round tower, grave slabs of monks, ancient walls and hut foundations – relics of the fifth-century monastery of Nendrum, one of Ireland's earliest Christian foundations, where St Patrick is said to have preached.

A massive grave slab, which many people believe marks St Patrick's burial place, lies just outside Downpatrick Cathedral

PLACES TO VISIT

Grey Abbey

➕ 197 F3 ☎ 028 4278 8585
🕐 Apr–Sep Tue–Sat 10–7, Sun 2–7; Oct–Mar Sat 10–4, Sun 2–4 💷 Free

Mount Stewart

➕ 197 F3 ☎ 028 4278 8387;
www.nationaltrust.org.uk 🕐 House: Jul–Aug daily noon–6; Jun daily 1–6; May and Sep Wed–Mon 1–6; early Mar–Apr and Oct Sat–Sun noon–6. Formal gardens: May–Sep daily 10–8; Apr and Oct daily 10–6; Mar daily 10–4. Lakeside gardens and walks: Daily 10–dusk. Temple of the Winds: Apr–Oct Sun 2–5 💷 Moderate

Castle Ward

➕ 197 F3 ☎ 028 4488 1204;
www.nationaltrust.org.uk 🕐 House: Jul–Aug daily 1–6; Apr–Jun and Sep Sat–Sun 1–6. Grounds: Apr–Sep daily 10–8; Oct–Mar 10–4 💷 Moderate

Quoile Countryside Centre

➕ 197 F3 ☎ 028 4461 5520;
www.ehsni.gov.uk/quoile 🕐 Apr–Aug daily 11–5; Sep–Mar Sat–Sun 1–5 💷 Free

Practicalities

BEFORE YOU GO

WHAT YOU NEED

	Some countries require a passport to remain valid for a minimum period (usually at least six months) beyond the date of entry – check before booking.	UK	Germany	USA	Canada	Australia	Ireland	Netherlands	Spain
● Required ○ Suggested ▲ Not required									
Passport/National Identity Card		▲	●	●	●	●	▲	●	●
Visa (regulations can change, please check)		▲	▲	▲	▲	▲	▲	▲	▲
Onward or Return Ticket		○	○	○	○	○	○	▲	○	○
Health Inoculations		▲	▲	▲	▲	▲	▲	▲	▲
Health Documentation (▶ 192, Health)		●	●	●	●	●	▲	●	●
Travel Insurance		○	○	○	○	○	○	○	○
Driving Licence (national)		●	●	●	●	●	●	●	●
Car Insurance Certificate		●	●	n/a	n/a	n/a	●	●	●
Car Registration Document		●	●	n/a	n/a	n/a	●	●	●

WHEN TO GO

Dublin

High season   Low season

JAN	FEB	MAR	APR	MAY	JUN	JUL	AUG	SEP	OCT	NOV	DEC
46°F	46°F	50°F	55°F	59°F	64°F	68°F	66°F	63°F	57°F	50°F	46°F
8°C	8°C	10°C	13°C	15°C	18°C	20°C	19°C	17°C	14°C	10°C	8°C

☀ Sun   ☁ Cloud   🌧 Wet

Temperatures are the **average daily maximum** for each month. The best weather is in spring and early summer (April and June) when the countryside looks its best. Winter (November to March) can be dark, wet and dreary, especially in the mountainous west, but good-weather days can be magical. In high summer (July and August) the weather is changeable and often cloudy. Autumn (September and October) generally sees good weather. The cities are great places to visit at any time, regardless of the weather, and Christmas and New Year are particularly popular. It will almost certainly rain at some time during your stay, no matter when you visit. Be prepared, but try to accept the rain as the Irish do, as a "wet blessing".

GETTING ADVANCE INFORMATION

■ Tourism Ireland:
www.discoverireland.com
■ Northern Ireland Tourist
Board: www.nitb.com

In the Irish Republic
Dublin: ☎ 1 850 230330;
www.visitdublin.com
Tourism Ireland: ☎ 0800
039 7000

In Northern Ireland
Belfast: ☎ 02890 231221;
www.gotobelfast.com
Tourism Ireland ☎ 0800
039 7000

GETTING THERE

By Air Scheduled flights operate from Britain, mainland Europe and North America to Dublin, Cork, Knock, Shannon and Belfast. **Aer Lingus** (tel: 0870 876 5000; www.aerlingus.com) operates services from London and regional UK airports, many European countries and the US. **Ryanair** (tel: 0871 246 0000; www.ryanair.com) flies to Dublin from all over Britain and to Belfast from London Stansted, and **British Midlands Airways (bmi)** (tel: 0870 60 70 555; www.flybmi.com) from Heathrow to Dublin and Belfast. Check with your travel agent, the airlines or the Internet for details of other carriers. **Flying time to Dublin:** from mainland UK 1–2 hours, from Europe 2–4 hours, from USA/Canada 8–11 hours, from Australia/New Zealand 24-plus hours. **Flying time to Belfast:** from mainland UK 1–2 hours, from Europe 2–3 hours, from USA/Canada 8–11 hours, from Australia/New Zealand via London 24-plus hours.

By Sea Most ferry services **from Britain** arrive at Dun Laoghaire and Belfast. **Crossing times:** Holyhead–Dun Laoghaire 99 minutes by HSS fast ferry; Holyhead–Dublin 3 hours 45 minutes, or under 2 hours by fast ferry; Fishguard–Rosslare 3 hours 30 minutes; Swansea–Cork 10 hours; Stranraer–Belfast 3 hours 30 minutes, or 1 hour by SeaCat, 1 hour 45 minutes by HSS; Cairnryan–Larne 2 hours 15 minutes, or 1 hour by Jetliner; Campbelltown– Ballycastle 3 hours. There are also services **from France** to the Republic: Roscoff–Cork (15 hours); Cherbourg–Rosslare (18 hours). **Ferry companies** operating services to Ireland are **Irish Ferries** (tel: 0870 5171717), **Stena Lines** (tel: 0870 5707070) and **Brittany Ferries** (tel: 08703 665333).

TIME

Ireland is on Greenwich Mean Time (GMT) in winter, but one hour ahead of GMT from late March until late October.

CURRENCY AND FOREIGN EXCHANGE

Currency The monetary units are (in the Republic) the euro (€), and (in Northern Ireland) the pound sterling (£).

Euro: notes are issued in denominations of 5, 10, 20, 50, 100, 200 and 500 euros, and **coins** in denominations of 1 and 2 euros, and 1, 2, 5, 10, 20 and 50 euro cents.

Pounds sterling: notes are issued in £5, £10, £20 and £50 denominations and **coins** in 1p, 2p, 5p, 10p, 20p, 50p, £1 and £2 denominations by the Bank of England, and in notes of £5, £10, £20 and £50 by the provincial banks. Provincial bank notes are not accepted in other parts of the UK. There are 100 pence in each pound.

Sterling or US dollar **travellers' cheques** are the most convenient way to carry money. All major **credit cards** are recognised.

Exchange Currency exchange bureaux are common in Dublin, Belfast, at airports, sea ports and some rail stations. They often operate longer hours but offer poorer rates of exchange than banks. Many banks have ATMs for cash withdrawals; check with your bank for details.

In mainland UK
☎ 0800 039 7000

In the USA and Canada
☎ 1-800-223-6470

In Australia and New Zealand
☎ 02 9299 6177 (Sydney)
☎ 09 977 2255 (Auckland)

WHEN YOU ARE THERE

NATIONAL HOLIDAYS

1 Jan	New Year's Day
17 Mar	St Patrick's Day
Mar/Apr	Good Friday (RI)
Mar/Apr	Easter Monday
First Mon May	May Holiday
Last Mon May	Spring Holiday (NI)
First Mon Jun	June Holiday (RI)
12 Jul	Orangeman's Day (NI)
First Mon Aug	August Holiday (RI)
Last Mon Aug	Late Summer Holiday (NI)
Last Mon Oct	October Holiday (RI)
25 Dec/26 Dec	Christmas Day/Boxing Day

ELECTRICITY

The power supply is: 230 volts (RI); 240 volts (NI). Type of socket: 3-square-pin (UK type). Parts of the Republic also have 2-round-pin (continental type). Overseas visitors should bring an adaptor.

OPENING HOURS

○ Shops
● Offices
● Banks
● Post Offices
● Museums/Monuments
● Pharmacies

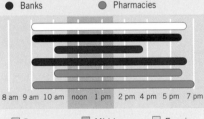

8 am 9 am 10 am noon 1 pm 2 pm 4 pm 5 pm 7 pm

☐ Day   ☐ Midday   ☐ Evening

Shops Some open until 8 or 9pm on Thursday and Friday. Smaller towns and rural areas have an early closing day (1pm) on one day a week.
Banks Nearly all banks are closed on Saturday. In smaller towns they may close for lunch.
Post Offices In rural areas post offices may close for lunch.

TIPS/GRATUITIES

Restaurants (service not included)	10%
Bar service	No
Tour guides	(RI) €3; (NI) £1
Hairdressers	(RI) €3; (NI) £1
Taxis	10%
Chambermaids	discretion
Porters	discretion
Lavatories	No

ROAD TRAVEL

Road signs are blue for motorways, green for major roads and white for local roads, but in the Republic distances are measured in kilometres and in Northern Ireland in miles. In RI roads signs have the Irish name first and English second, but in Northern Ireland are generally in English only.

TIME DIFFERENCES

GMT
12 noon

Ireland
12 noon

London
12 noon

←
USA (NY)
7am

←
USA (West Coast)
4am

Sydney
10pm

STAYING IN TOUCH

In the Republic, mail boxes and vans are painted green. You can buy stamps from post offices, machines or some newsstands. In the North, mail boxes and vans are red; British stamps are used and British postal rates apply.

Public telephones Telephone boxes are: (RI) cream, or green-and-white; (NI) red, or Perspex-and-metal booths. Payphones accept: (RI) 10, 20 and 50 cents and €1 coins; (NI) 10p, 20p, 50p and £1 coins. Callcards (RI) or phonecards (NI) are widely accepted, sold at post offices and newsstands. For the domestic operator, dial: (RI) 10; (NI) 100. For the international operator, dial: (RI) 114; (NI) 155.

International Dialling Codes
Dial 00 followed by

UK:	44		
(from RI only; no code from NI)			
USA/Canada:	1	Australia:	61
Germany:	49	Spain:	34

Mobile providers and services Most GSM phones can be used in Ireland but check with your provider that you have a roaming agreement. It might be less expensive to buy a cheap pay-as-you-go sim card on the spot and pay for calls at the local rate, and you can top it up when necessary. The main companies are Vodafone, O2, Meteor, 3 and Tesco Mobile.

Wi-Fi and Internet Wi-Fi internet access is now widely available in airports and hotels. Some hotels will charge a fee but most are free, and some have computer terminals for use by guests if you haven't brought your laptop. You'll find internet cafes in major cities and sometimes also in the local tourist information office.

PERSONAL SAFETY

The national police forces are:
RI – Garda Síochána (pronounced *sheekawnah*) in black-and-blue uniforms.
NI – Police Service of Northern Ireland (PSNI) in dark green uniforms.

- ■ Belfast is as safe as any modern city: observe your usual personal security precautions.
- ■ Take care of personal property in Dublin.
- ■ Avoid leaving property visible in cars.
- ■ Listen out for news alerts, as dissident activities occasionally disrupt train, bus and road travel in Northern Ireland and between Belfast and Dublin.
- ■ Don't leave bags/luggage unattended in public places as this can cause unnecessary security alerts.
- ■ If going walking in remote areas, make sure you take emergency food, drink, clothing and a mobile phone.

Police assistance:
☏ **999 or 112** from any phone (RI)
☏ **999** from any phone (NI)

HEALTH

 Insurance Citizens of EU countries receive free or reduced-cost emergency medical treatment with relevant documentation (European Health Insurance Card), although private medical insurance is still advised, and is essential for all other visitors.

 Dental Services EU nationals, or nationals of other countries with which Ireland has a reciprocal agreement, can get reduced dental treatment within the Irish health service with an EHIC card (not needed for UK nationals). Others should take out private medical insurance.

 Weather The sunniest months are May and June (average 5–7 hours of sun a day in the southeast), although July and August are the hottest. During these months you should cover up, use a good sunscreen and drink plenty of fluids.

 Drugs and Medicines Prescription and non-prescription drugs are available from pharmacies. Pharmacists can advise on medication for common ailments. When closed, most pharmacies display notices giving details of the nearest one that is open.

 Safe Water Tap water is safe to drink. Mineral water is widely available but is often expensive, particularly in restaurants.

CONCESSIONS

Students Holders of an International Student Identity Card can buy a Travelsave Stamp which entitles them to travel discounts including a 50 per cent reduction on Bus Éireann, Iarnród Éireann and Irish Ferries (between Britain and Ireland). Contact a student travel agency for further details. The Travelsave Stamp can be purchased from USIT, 19–21 Aston Quay, O'Connell Bridge, Dublin 2 (tel: 01 602 1904).
Senior Citizens Discounts on transport and admission fees are usually available on proof of age.

TRAVELLING WITH A DISABILITY

Increasing numbers of hotels and other public buildings are being adapted or specially built to cater for travellers with disabilities. For information on travelling with a disability useful contacts are: National Disability Authority, 25 Clyde Road, Dublin 4 ☎ 01 608 0400; www.nda.ie. For Northern Ireland: Disability Action ☎ 028 9029 7880; www.disabilityaction.org.

CHILDREN

Well-behaved children are generally made welcome everywhere. Public houses operate individual admittance policies. In the North there are designated areas for children in most pubs. Concessions on transport and entrance fees are available.

LAVATORIES

Public lavatories are usually clean and safe. Some are coin-entry, others are free.

SMOKING

Ireland banned smoking in the workplace in 2004. This means you cannot light up in restaurants or pubs, but hotels may have designated smoking rooms.

EMBASSIES AND CONSULATES

UK
01 205 3700 (RI)

USA
01 668 8777 (RI)
028 9032 8239 (NI)

Australia
01 664 5300 (RI)
020 7379 4334 (NI)

Canada
01 417 4100 (RI)
020 7258 6600 (NI)

Germany
01 269 3011 (RI)
020 7824 1300 (NI)

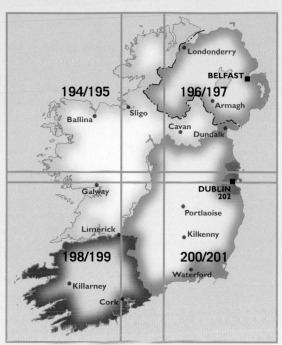

To identify the regions see the map on the inside of the front cover

Regional Maps

––––––––	International boundary	▢	Capital city
═══════	Motorway	▫	Town/village
────────	Major route	◼	Featured place of interest
────────	Main road	▪	Place of interest
────────	Other road	✈	Airport
	Built-up area	▲	Height in metres

194-201 0 ———————————— 40 km
0 ———————————— 30 miles

Streetplan

––––––	Main road/minor road	◼	Featured place of interest
▪	Important building		Park/garden

202 0 ———————————— 400 metres
0 ———————————— 400 yards

Atlas

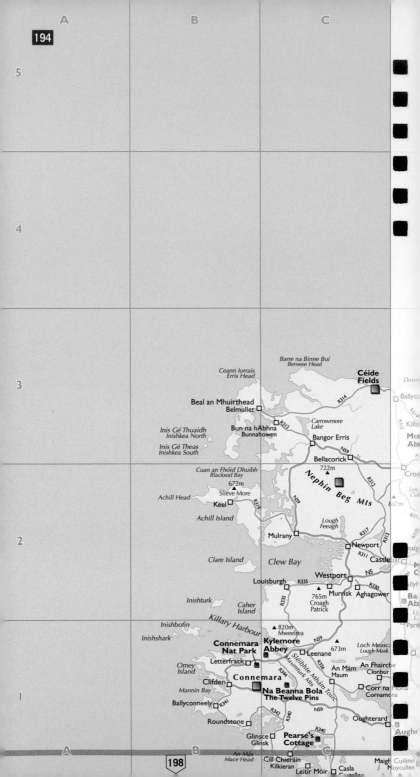

5

4

3

Barre na Binne Buí
Benwee Head
Ceann Iorrais
Erris Head
**Céide
Fields**

R314

Dow

Beal an Mhuirthead
Belmullet

R313

Ballyc

Carrowmore
Lake

R315

Killa

Bun na hAbhna
Bunnahowen

Bangor Erris

N59

Inis Gé Thuaidh
Inishkea North

Mo
Ab

Inis Gé Theas
Inishkea South

Bellacorick

Cuan an Fhóid Dhuibh
Blacksod Bay

722m

Nephin Beg Mts

R312

Cros

Lo
C

672m
Slieve More

R319

N59

807m

R31

Achill Head

Keel

Achill Island

Lough
Feeagh

R317

R312

Mulrany

2

Clare Island

Clew Bay

Newport

R311

Castle

bar

N5

Westport

ou

M
C

Louisburgh

R335

R330

ly

R335

Murrisk Aghagower

Ba
Ab

765m
Croagh
Patrick

Inishturk

Caher
Island

Lo
C

Par

Killary Harbour

Inishbofin

820m
Mweelrea

**Connemara
Nat Park**

**Kylemore
Abbey**

673m

*Loch Measca
Lough Mask*

Inishshark

N59

1

Omey
Island

Letterfrack

*Sléibhte Mhám Toirc
Maumturk Mts*

Leenane

An Fhairche
Clonbur

fl na

Clifden

Connemara

R344

An Mám
Maum

R336

Corr na
Cornamona

Mona
Ab

Mannin Bay

**Na Beanna Bola
The Twelve Pins**

Ballyconneely

R341

R340

R340

N59

Oughterard

Aughr

Roundstone

Glinsce
Glinsk

**Pearse's
Cottage**

An Más
Mace Head

Cill Chiaráin
Kilkieran

Leitir Móir

Casla
Co

Maigh

Cuilinn
Moycullen

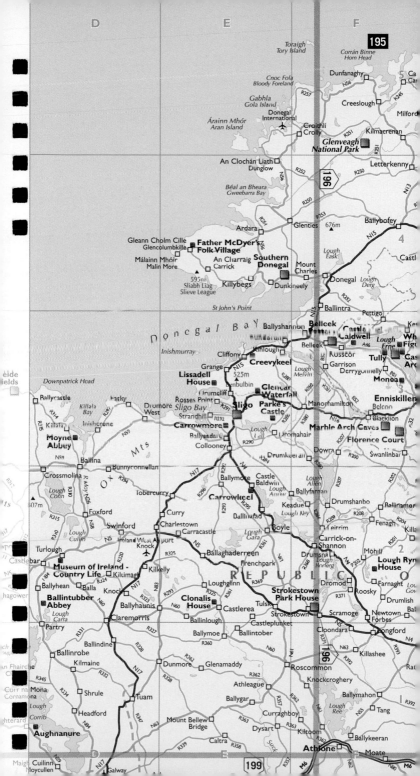

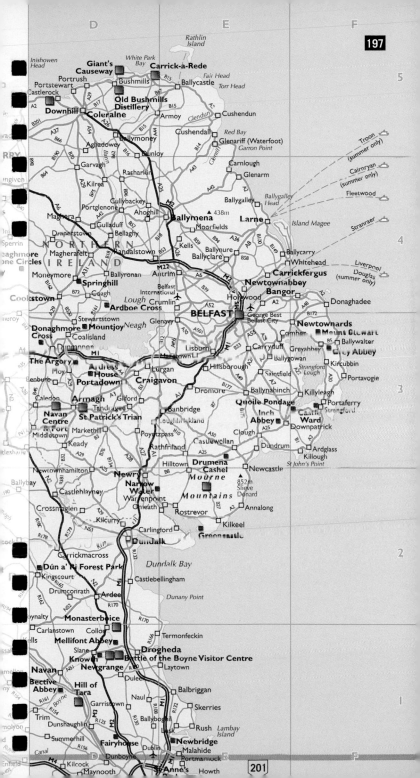

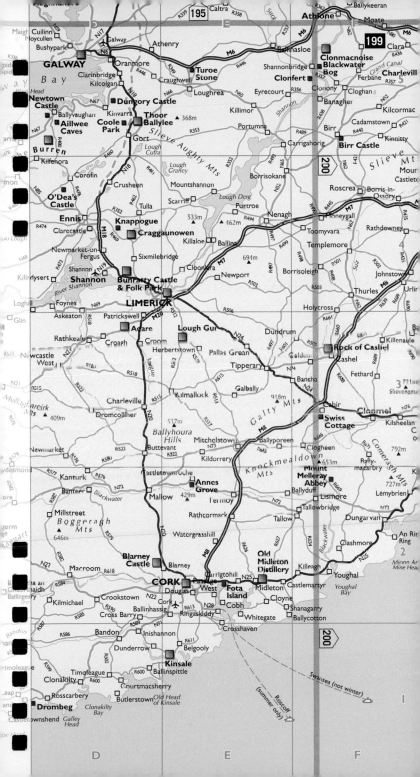

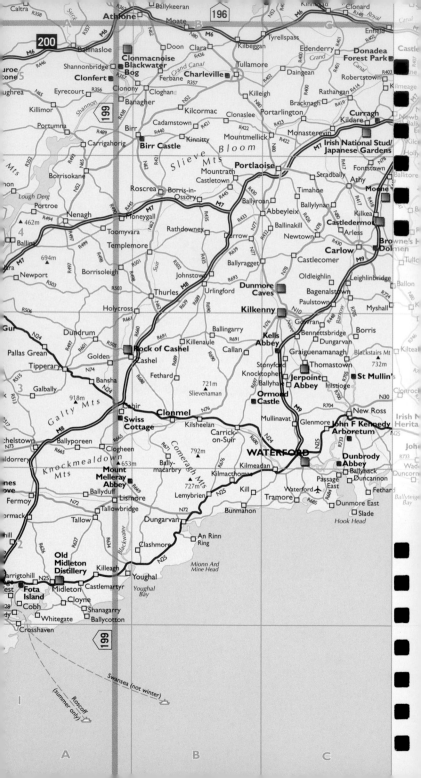

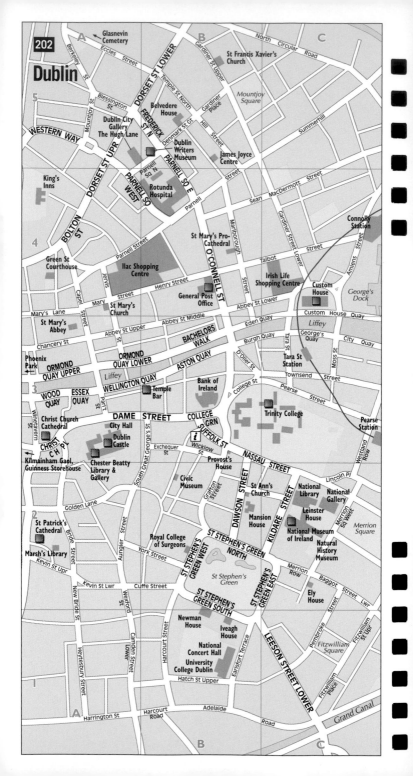

Picture credits

Abbreviations for terms appearing below: (t) top; (b) bottom; (l) left; (r) right; (c) centre.

The Automobile Association wishes to thank the following photographers, libraries and organizations for their assistance in the preparation of this book.

2t AA/S McBride; 2c AA/C Jones; 2c AA/S Day; 2b AA/M Short; 3t AA/D Forss; 3c AA/C Coe; 3c AA/C Coe; 3b AA/L Blake; 5l AA/S McBride; 5c AA/S Day; 5r AA/C Jones; 7 Alamy/Elizabeth Leyden; 8–9 Getty Images/Michael Cooper; 9 Getty Images/Julian Herbert; 11 Alamy/Stephen Emerson; 13tl Alamy/Classic Image; 13tr Alamy/Ivy Close Images; 15t Mary Evans Picture Library; 15c Mary Evans Picture Library; 15b Alamy/ North Wind Picture Archives; 17t AA/Chris Close; 17c Mary Evans Picture Library/ILN Pictures; 17b PA Photos/PA Archive/ Rui Vieira; 18 TopFoto/ HIP/ The Print Collector; 19 Getty Images/Topical Press Agency; 20 AA/C Jones; 21 Getty Images AFP/ Paul Faith; 23 Fairyhouse Racecourse; 25 Robert Harding Picture Library/Gary Cook; 26 Corbis/ Sergio Pitamitz; 27 Rex Features/OSD Photo Agency; 28 Rex Features/Tony Kyriacou; 29 Alamy/ David Sanger Photography; 30–31t Bridgeman Art Library/Sir John Lavery/Crawford Municipal Art Gallery, Cork, Ireland; 30c Alamy/Religion UK/Alan King; 32 Getty Images; 33l AA/C Jones; 33c AA/C Jones; 33r AA/C Jones; 45l AA/S Day; 45c AA/S Day; 45r AA/S McBride; 46 AA/S Whitehorne; 48cr AA/S Day; 48b AA/S Day; 49 AA/S Day; 51 The Bridgeman Art Library/The Board of Trinity College, Dublin, Ireland; 52t AA/S McBride; 52b Illustrated London News; 53 AA/S McBride; 54 The Bridgeman Art Library/National Museum of Ireland, Dublin, Ireland/Boltin Picture Library; 55 AA/S Day; 56 The Bridgeman Art Library/National Museum of Ireland, Dublin, Ireland/Boltin Picture Library; 57 Photolibrary/The Irish Image Collection; 58–59 AA/S Whitehorne; 60 AA/S Day; 63 Photolibrary/The Irish Image Collection; 64 Photolibrary/ The Irish Image Collection; 71l AA/ M Short; 71c AA/C Jones; 71r AA/M Short; 74c AA/M Short; 74b AA/C Coe; 75 Alamy/Arco Images GmbH; 76 Scenic Ireland/Chris Hill; 78-79 AA/S McBride; 79t Photolibrary/imagebroker.net/ Christian Handl; 80 AA/C Jones; 81 AA/P Zollier; 82t AA/C Jones; 82-83b AA/C Jones; 83c AA/ C Jones; 84 AA/C Coe; 85 Photolibrary/The Irish Image Collection; 86 AA/M Short; 87 Corbis/ Destinations; 88 Battle of Boyne Visitor Centre; 93l AA/D Forss; 93c AA/S Hill; 93r AA/J Blandford; 96 AA/C Jones; 97 AA/C Jones; 98 AA/C Jones; 99 AA/C Jones; 100 AA/S McBride; 101 AA/ S McBride; 102/103 AA/S McBride; 102c AA/S Hill; 104-105b AA/S Day; 105t AA/C Jones; 106 AA/C Jones; 107 AA/C Jones; 108 Alamy /David Kilpatrick; 109 AA/S Hill; 110 Alamy/David Noton Photography; 111 AA/P Zollier; 112t AA/D Forss; 112b Alamy/George Munday; 119l AA/C Coe; 119c AA/S Hill; 119r Scenic Ireland/Paul Lindsay; 121t AA/C Coe; 121b AA/S Day; 122c AA/ M Diggin; 122b AA/S Hill; 123t AA/C Coe; 123b AA/C Hill; 124 AA/S Hill; 125 NHPA /David Wood-fall; 126 AA/S McBride; 127 NHPA/Robert Thompson; 128 AA/S Hill; 129 AA/S Hill; 130 AA/ L Blake; 131 AA/C Jones; 132 AA/C Coe; 133 AA/L Blake; 134 AA/P Zollier; 135 AA/S McBride; 136 AA/M Diggin; 137 AA/I Dawson; 138 AA/C Coe; 145l AA/C Coe; 145c AA/C Coe; 145r AA; 148c Scenic Ireland/Chris Hill; 148b AA/G Munday; 149 Scenic Ireland/Chris Hill; 150 AA/C Coe; 151 AA/C Coe; 152 AA/C Coe; 153 Alamy/Joe Fox; 154 AA/C Coe; 155 National Trust NI/John Lennon; 156 AA/C Coe; 157 AA/C Coe; 158 AA/C Coe; 159 AA; 160 AA/J Johnson; 161 AA/C Coe; 162 AA/ G Munday; 163 AA/G Munday; 164 AA/C Coe; 165 Alamy/The National Trust/Derek Croucher; 166 Alamy/scenicireland.com/Christopher Hill Photographic; 171l AA/L Blake; 171c AA/C Coe; 171r AA/M Short; 173 AA/S Whitehorne; 176 Alamy/Andrew McConnell; 177 Alamy/ LOOK Die Bildagentur der Fotografen GmbH ; 179c AA/C Coe; 179r AA/C Hill; 182 AA/C Coe; 183 Alamy/ David Lyons; 184 AA/I Dawson; 185 AA/G Munday; 186 AA/G Munday; 187l AA/C Jones; 187c AA/ C Jones; 187r AA/I Dawson; 191t AA/C Jones; 191c AA/C Jones; 191b AA/C Jones.

Acknowledgements

The author would like to thank John Lahiffe and Katrina Doherty of the Irish Tourist Board for their help during the research of this book.